THE NORTHUMBRIAN PUB

an architectural history

LYNN F. PEARSON

B.Sc. M.A. Ph.D. M.Litt.

SANDHILL
PRESS

First published in Great Britain in 1989
by Sandhill Press Ltd., 17 Castle Street,
Warkworth, Morpeth,
Northumberland, NE65 0UW

Copyright © Lynn F. Pearson

ISBN 0 946098 15 8

Designed by Janet Dickson, Alnwick.
Printed by Martin's of Berwick, and bound by Hunter & Foulis, Edinburgh.

CONTENTS

FIGURES

PLATES

Colour Plates

Note: Colour plates 1, 6, 7, 8, 9 and 17 by Les Golding.

Drinking in the North East

THE Northumbrian public house in its many varieties is the outcome of a complex chain of events centred on the brewing industry but involving financiers and traders, architects and builders, which came to a head around the turn of the nineteenth century. The surviving pubs built during the late Victorian and Edwardian building boom are not merely buildings but constant reminders of fashionable artistic taste, of high quality craft skills, of architectural showmanship and, crucially, of the great investment made by the brewing industry in buildings as a means of attracting customers.

Although many exciting pubs have been demolished, enough remain to show that national architectural trends were reflected in pub building, that good local architects produced excellent pub designs, and that north eastern pubs have a particular identity, quite different from that of the more famous grand Victorian pubs of London, or the terracotta pubs of Birmingham. The local economic situation was of vital importance to brewers when decisions were taken about building or, more often, rebuilding urban pubs; North Shields and Sunderland in particular still have clear evidence in pub form of their economic ups and downs. This book attempts to gather together strands of information on architecture, brewers, the local economy and social history and, through the buildings themselves, explain why north eastern pubs look as they do today. Urban pubs, country pubs, pubs now demolished, all form part of this story, which reaches in time from the Georgian era to the present day and beyond.

Investigating buildings is made simpler by the fact that a great deal of archival evidence still exists relating to their architects and original plans. This material is often to be found in county record offices, and has been used as the basis of the pub diagrams which show the outline of the ground floor of the building, interior walls and the bar counter. Using these plans and diagrams, and the evidence of the buildings themselves, it is possible to trace changes in drinking habits and relate these to national trends in the nineteenth and early twentieth centuries.

This book is not a comprehensive guide to the pubs of the north east, but it is a guide to the main movements in pub architecture and the styles of local pub architects, most of whom were also well known for their commercial and ecclesiastical buildings. Those interested in finding out more about their local pub will do well to begin at their local record office, where building control plans are the first step in any investigation. The most important piece of evidence is often the pub itself, where social and architectural pleasures can often be combined in contemplation of the delights of Victorian joinery or Edwardian tilework!

Any piece of historical research is dependent upon the availability of relevant archival material and also the hard work of archivists, and I am extremely grateful to all the archivists whose patience I tested during 1988, particularly those of the Tyne and Wear Archives Service who unfailingly produced plan after plan for me to inspect. I would like to thank all those individuals and organisations who helped with this research, by suggesting interesting pubs, by giving permission for illustrations to be reproduced, or by letting me consult their archival material: Sue and John Constable (of the Chain Locker, New Quay, North Shields), Mrs. C.A. Danes, Mr K. Draper (of the Half Moon, New Elvet, Durham), Sue Hudson, Jane Lamont, Mr. J.C. Lane, Miss E. Milburn, Simon Parton, Alan W. T. Railston, Mr G. T. Stewart, British Rail (Eastern), CAMRA (Tyneside Branch), Scottish and Newcastle Breweries, University of Newcastle upon Tyne School of Education, Durham County Record Office (at Durham and Darlington), Gateshead Libraries and Arts Department, Ironbridge Gorge Museum Trust, Newcastle upon Tyne City Library, North Tyneside Local Studies Centre, North Tyneside Planning Department, Northumberland Record Office, Sunderland Museum and Art Gallery, (Tyne and Wear Museums Service), Tyne and Wear Archives Service (illustrations reproduced by kind permission of the Chief Archivist, the City Engineer of the City of Newcastle upon Tyne and the Director of Engineering, Sunderland Borough Council). I would also like to acknowledge the contribution made by the City Engineer's Department of the City of Newcastle upon Tyne to the preservation of the plans, prior to them coming within the care of the Tyne and Wear Archives Service. And not forgetting Boots the dog.

Lynn F. Pearson
Gosforth, Newcastle upon Tyne
October 1988

CHAPTER ONE

The City Pub

Newcastle upon Tyne's Market Streets

I N 1882 the United Kingdom Alliance, a temperance organisation founded in 1853 to work towards the prohibition of the liquor trade, produced a map of Newcastle showing all the licensed premises. 446 fully licensed houses, the equivalent of today's public houses, were marked as well as another 324 beerhouses, 36 breweries and 77 off-licences, making a total of 883 places at which alcohol could be bought. As the map shows (see Fig. 1), the small area centred on the Town Hall and including the Bigg, Cloth and Groat Markets contained 23 pubs and 4 beerhouses; in 1778 there had been 11 pubs while in 1837 the total was 17, the increase reflecting the rising population of Newcastle in the nineteenth century and the mid-Victorian rise in beer consumption. British beer production topped 30 million barrels a year in the late 1870s, with weekly consumption averaging out at over five pints per head for every man, woman and child. The brewing industry expanded and changed as its market grew, with small, local brewers giving way to larger firms who distributed their products more widely. From the 1880s onwards, the situation changed with the

level of real wages increasing but individual beer consumption remaining fairly constant; people were finding other ways of spending their spare time and money. Competition within the brewing industry heightened and battles were fought over the humble city pub, previously little more than a room with a counter and perhaps a few seats. By the turn of the century it had become the focal point of the sales war between the brewers, wine and spirit merchants and other pub owners, and had been turned into a showplace for the brewers' products. Not all city pubs were changed, of course; there were those which stayed, little affected, in the hands of a single family for many years, but the story of the pubs in the Bigg Market area of Newcastle illustrates very well the attempts of the brewers and other related companies to keep their share of the market.

It is a complex story involving the sale and resale of many pubs, their alteration at the hands of numerous architects, a high turnover of licensees and constant changes in brands of beer as breweries amalgamated or developed new brews in the attempt to keep up consumption. It resulted in similarly

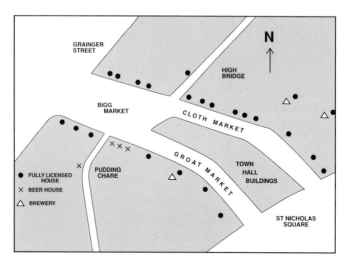

1. Licensed premises around the Town Hall, Newcastle, 1882
(Newcastle upon Tyne City Library)

complex pubs, many of which have disappeared or undergone enormous alterations, but enough remain to give some indication of their spectacular interiors. Fortunately many of the plans and drawings from this late Victorian and Edwardian boom in pub building have been preserved. The story of the drink trade and the pubs in the Bigg Market area can best be told by examining the history of a few of these pubs in detail, beginning with the Lord Chancellor in Groat Market. Today this is better known as Maceys, its interior completely modernised, but in 1892 it had one of the most interesting and advanced interiors of any Newcastle pub.

MACEYS – THE LORD CHANCELLOR
31 Groat Market

The interior of the Lord Chancellor about a century

ago was typical of many pubs in the Bigg, Cloth and Groat markets, being long and narrow with a front bar, a rear select bar and two sitting rooms (see Fig. 2). It was separated from the neighbouring White Horse Inn (now the site of Thomson House) by Ridley Court, and had been owned since at least the early 1870s by an unmarried Glasgow lady, Elizabeth Davison. Its tenants in the early 1880s were Mr and Mrs Elsbury, but the wine and spirit merchants S. Oliver & Co. took over the tenancy in 1892, and immediately submitted plans to the Town Improvement Committee for alterations and enlargement of the pub. Before 1892 the Elsburys had probably run a free house, meaning that they had a free choice when deciding which beers to sell, rather than a tied house where the licensee sold the beer of one particular brewer or wine and spirit merchant. The free house was either owned by the

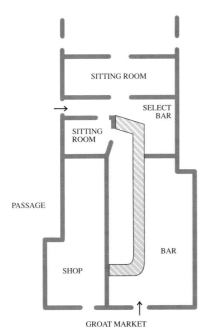

*2. Lord Chancellor, pre-1892;
(from TWA T186/14878)*

licensee or rented from a non-brewer or wine merchant. There were various forms of tied house; in London, where property prices were high and many pubs were leasehold, brewers often lent new tenants the money to buy the lease and make any 'goodwill' payment required, these pubs then being loan-tied to the brewery. More usually, a tied house was owned by a brewer or wine merchant and rented by the licensee, another arrangement being that the brewer or merchant supplied a loan at a preferential rate for the mortgage on a property. The Elsburys might also have brewed their own beer, but this is unlikely as only 10% of publicans brewed their own beer in the

late 1880s; by 1891, in the whole of the Tyneside area there were only three publicans who possessed a licence to brew.

What sort of beer would the Elsburys have sold at the Lord Chancellor in the late 1880s? It would not have been the traditional Newcastle Mild, a strong, sweet, dark ale brewed on Tyneside using poor quality local water and barley; this was the only beer available in most pubs in the 1860s but pale ales from Burton and Scotland had almost completely replaced it by 1890. The Burton brewers, particularly Bass and Allsopp, dramatically expanded production of their clear, sparkling, light ales in the mid-nineteenth century, Bass building two new breweries between 1850 and 1865. Their beer became popular in the north east because of its high quality compared with local brews, and at first was sold not through tied houses but a system of beer agents, often wine and spirit merchants who contracted to sell beer from non-Tyneside brewers to the local retail trade. Scottish beer, also clearer and lighter than the local brews, increased in popularity at the same time, the brewers again using the agency system to promote sales. Beer agents could themselves be brewers, as in the case of W. B. Reid & Co. of the Leazes Brewery in Newcastle, who became agents for William Younger of Edinburgh in the mid- nineteenth century and after many changes were finally taken over by them in 1956. The Tyneside market was very important to the Scottish brewers, most of whom had agencies on Tyneside by 1870. William Younger & Co. was selling a third of its output here by 1890, and around the turn of the century about a quarter of the production of Scotland's six leading brewers was destined for this area.

The invasion of Tyneside by the Scottish and Burton brewers led to a different pattern of pub ownership from that common in London or Birmingham. On Tyneside, the marketing of the new, clear ales provided strong competition for local brewers from around the 1860s. In order to retain their sales outlets and attempt to fight off the newcomers the local brewers began to buy the freeholds of pubs, the licensees then being tied to their products or those for which the brewer was an agent. The tied pubs also provided an immediate outlet for clear ales which the local brewers began to develop as a response to the new Scottish and Burton ales. The wine and spirit merchants joined in the freehold buying, to defend their agency sales, and by the early 1870s local brewers and wine and spirit merchants owned a considerable number of pubs, up to a third of the total in the All Saints parish (between Byker and the city centre), for example. Although this process took longer in the city centre, it still occurred earlier than in other parts of England where competition from non-local brewers was less intense and freehold purchasing happened from the 1880s onwards. Scottish and other non-Tyneside brewers bought pubs in Newcastle in the 1880s, and as the number of available pubs fell, the new owners had to think of other means of attracting and keeping custom. If they couldn't buy new pubs, at least they could change the image of the old pubs by fitting them out with sparkling mirrors, carved and curving bar counters and totally new and grandiose facades. This late nineteenth century burst of pub modernisation changed the face of the city, and provided us with the idea of the typical Victorian pub which we retain today.

In 1897, at the peak of the boom in central Newcastle, 63 applications were made to alter or rebuild public houses. From a trickle in the 1860s, pub rebuilding had accelerated to a lesser peak of 45 applications in 1890 and hit a trough in 1895 before rising rapidly to the 1897 level, a pattern similar to events in London where brewers warred throughout the 1890s until property prices crashed in 1899. Applications tended to come from local firms around 1890 and non-local or amalgamated firms in 1899. Although rebuilding applications in Newcastle declined sharply after 1897, there was still a substantial amount of building activity in the early twentieth century, 24 applications in 1905 for instance. The relatively healthy state of the pub property market on Tyneside was probably the outcome of the variety in pub ownership, with brewers, wine and spirit merchants, publicans and many individual investors owning pubs. The biggest holding of pubs in Newcastle in 1890 was that of the Richard Grainger estate, Grainger being the builder and developer of a large part of the city centre in the 1820s-30s. The estate held 35 pubs at that time and sold none in the central Newcastle parishes of St Nicholas and St John between 1872 and 1915. Other landowners eventually sold out to the trade but the process was slow, giving stability to the market. Just over one hundred pubs were licensed throughout the 1872-1915 period in these two parishes, and even with the great demand for pubs by the trade, half of these were still in individual or estate ownership in 1915, compared to a national figure of 90% of pubs owned by brewers in 1900.

Wine and spirit merchants Oliver & Co. were rather behind the times when they acquired the tenancy of the Lord Chancellor in 1892, other merchants having been in the business of licensees, as owners or tenants, from the 1870s. As if to remedy this they immediately set about changing the appearance of the pub, engaging no less an architect than Benjamin F. Simpson of Grey Street to draw up the plans. Simpson's best known building in Newcastle is the bubbling art nouveau tower of Emerson Chambers, built by his partnership in 1904 just to the north of the Monument. His new design for the Lord Chancellor had an unexceptional facade, a door either side of a long window split into two by a central support, with some decoration in the form of panelling below it. The real attraction of the pub was its interior, transformed from a set of rooms with a plain bar counter to a complex arrangement of rooms and screens (see Fig. 3). As before there were four separate drinking areas, but now all had direct access to the bar, which itself had become an almost continuous rectangle in the centre of the building. Most unusual of all, the rear select bar was divided by screens into three distinct areas, with snob screens on the counter preventing customers from seeing into adjacent parts of the bar, and the publican from observing the customers. The snob screens were often highly decorative, with carved wood and engraved glass, and left just enough room above the counter for serving; more sophisticated snob screens had panels which swivelled to give the publican a view of the bar.

The Lord Chancellor's four rooms, six if the screened areas of the select bar are all counted, were something of an innovation on Tyneside, where the typical bar tended to be a long room with a single counter, with a further room to the rear. Modernisation of this type of pub often meant no more than extending the service area of the bar

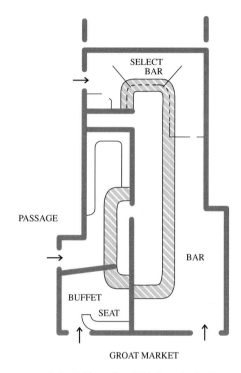

3. Lord Chancellor, 1892 design by B. F. Simpson; (from TWA T186/14878)

counter, producing a long bar with few, if any screens. This 'long bar' system was criticised in 1896 when John Roberts, Clerk to the Justices for Newcastle, told the Royal Commission on the Liquor Licensing Laws that it unduly encouraged drinking. He suggested that men would enter a pub and instead of having a drink or two in a well-screened bar and then leaving, would be able to see their friends in all parts of the pub and would therefore feel forced to buy extra rounds of drinks. Simpson's plan for the Lord Chancellor combined efficient service from a central counter with screened areas, a design which had already begun to be outmoded in London where compartmented pubs had been fashionable in the 1880s.

Although Oliver & Co. must have made a considerable investment in the Lord Chancellor, they only kept the tenancy for four years until 1896, when it was taken over by George White & Co., another local firm of wine and spirit merchants who were beginning to expand their number of outlets. They were tenants or owners of four Newcastle pubs by 1899, and kept the Lord Chancellor until 1913, when it became the focus of a complex arrangement of leasing and tenancy on the part of two brewers and its owners, the Vinycomb family of Newcastle and Belfast, who had bought the freehold in 1906. In 1913 James Calder & Co., Alloa, Ltd., took out a lease on the pub, as they also did on the Queen's Hotel in Clayton Street, leasing it from the executors of the Richard Grainger estate on one of the few occasions when the estate relinquished direct control of any of its property. Calder were brewers at the Shore Brewery in Alloa, but instead of running the pub themselves, the local brewers Robinson & Anderson were installed as tenants, presumably selling their own and Calder's beer; in effect they were acting as agents. The pub was left unchanged until 1928 when the screens and counter in the bar and select bar were demolished to make way for an extension of what was to be called the public bar. The buffet was left unchanged but the fine Victorian select bar counter disappeared, to be replaced by a semi-oval counter in an open, L-shaped room. The more spacious bar suited the streamlined thirties, when Victorian styles were anathema to progressive designers, and the plan

survived until after the war.

Robinson & Anderson also survived until 1948, one of the last of the local breweries to avoid takeover or amalgamation. The battle between the breweries for control of tied houses led to an increasing number of amalgamations and takeovers in the 1890s, the most famous local example being the formation of Newcastle Breweries Ltd. in 1890 from four firms: Newcastle's John Barras & Co. Ltd., J. J. & W. H. Allison & Co., and Carr Bros. and Carr, both of North Shields, and Gateshead's Swinburne & Co. The constituent firms brought with them their tied houses, and by the end of 1897 the new firm owned or had an interest in 318 pubs in the north-east, following further acquisitions. Another local amalgamation resulted in the formation of W. B. Reid & Co. Ltd. in 1891, the value of their properties in 1894 representing 84% of their capital. The process of concentration of brewing and pub ownership into fewer hands continued throughout the twentieth century, although rather more slowly than in the frantic 1890s. Consumption of beer declined after the First World War to a new weekly low of just over two pints per head, less than half the late 1870s figure, just before the Second World War. Further post-war mergers saw the advent of the giant national brewing groups, and Robinson & Anderson were caught up in these activities. In 1948 they were taken over by Hammond's United Breweries Ltd. of Bradford, although a 1950 plan for changes to the Lord Chancellor retains the Robinson & Anderson name. This time, the whole of the pub was to be remodelled, leaving a small central serving counter in a large open bar space, with a buffet bar to the rear. The only remaining vestige of Simpson's 1892 design was the curved window seat fronting on to Groat Market.

Hammond's became a part of Northern Breweries Ltd. in 1959, this company also taking in John Jeffrey & Co. Ltd. who had supplied beer to Calder pubs after Calder & Co. stopped brewing in 1951. Calder, who leased the Lord Chancellor in 1913, were themselves taken over by Northern Breweries in 1960, which eventually became part of the Bass Charrington group. In its current incarnation as Maceys, the twinkling lights of Victorian times have returned but the interior with its light well is quite different from all previous designs; only the bar counter, set at right angles to the street, is reminiscent of the pre-1892 design. The interior has been rebuilt at least four times, each new plan attempting to attract more trade; this is the one constant theme throughout the story of the city centre pubs and their owners.

THE HALF MOON
14 Bigg Market

Although the High Victorian interior of the Lord Chancellor is long gone, the work of the architect Benjamin Simpson can be seen much as it was intended in the facade of the Half Moon, built in 1904 in nearby Bigg Market (see Plate 1). The decorative and imposing facade of this grade II listed building shows the strength of the Scottish brewing invasion of Tyneside, as it was commissioned shortly after Archibald Arrol & Sons Ltd. of Alloa took over the pub. The Half Moon is a significant pub in the history of the north-east drink trade, as it was the headquarters of the brewing, wine and spirit company Meikle & Deuchar. The four Deuchar

1. Half Moon

brothers left Scotland as young men, James and George going into partnership with James and John Meikle in 1868, and Robert and Alexander becoming innkeepers. Robert took over a brewery in 1890, and Robert Deuchar & Co. Ltd. eventually built up a large estate of tied houses before the company was taken over by Newcastle Breweries Ltd. in 1953. James and George Deuchar left the

Meikle and Deuchar business in 1880; George took no further part in the drink trade but James formed a company which was also taken over by Newcastle Breweries Ltd. three years after his brother's company in 1956. The Meikle part of the business remained at the Half Moon, John Meikle taking over the ownership of the pub after the death of James in 1883.

Meikle expanded his tied estate to 11 pubs in Newcastle by 1892, but in 1895 he and William Turnbull, another Newcastle brewer who also owned a few pubs, both became part of the new company formed by Arrol the Alloa brewers. Arrols had sold their products on Tyneside from before 1870, but this was their first step into the tied house market, brought about by the increased competition in the industry around the turn of the century; the company later expanded its holdings by taking leases on more pubs in the early years of the following century.

Before the Arrol merger, Meikle's Half Moon had been a plain brick three storey building with two ground floor bars, its only external decoration being the name of its owner in large capitals above the central front door. Simpson's first redesign of the pub in November 1895 didn't change the facade a great deal, adding only decorative pilasters and lights over the windows, but the interior of the front bar was to be totally transformed by fitting it out with a circular bar counter (see Fig. 4). Arrols, however, thought again and commissioned a complete rebuilding in 1903, again by Simpson. This second chance enabled Simpson, by now showing the influence of the Glasgow architect Charles Rennie Mackintosh, to go for a five storey Art Nouveau frontage. A niche in the uppermost part of the central scrolled gable

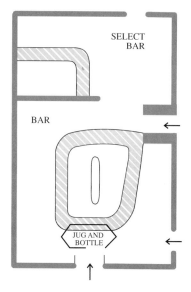

4. Half Moon, 1895 design by B. F. Simpson (not built); (from TWA T186/16747)

contained a crescent moon, probably modelled in stone, but this has now disappeared. Behind the dramatic facade Simpson toyed with the idea of a U-shaped bar counter but finally settled on a rounded rectangle for the front bar (see Plate 2), the rear select bar being turned into a sitting room. When the pub reopened in 1905 (the date is inscribed over the unused entrance on Bigg Market) this plan gave the new landlord, one Mr Richards, four separate spaces in the front bar, all served from the central island counter, a highly efficient arrangement. Little remains of Simpson's interior except a mirror surround at the rear, in what would have been the sitting room.

The new facade also commemorated the

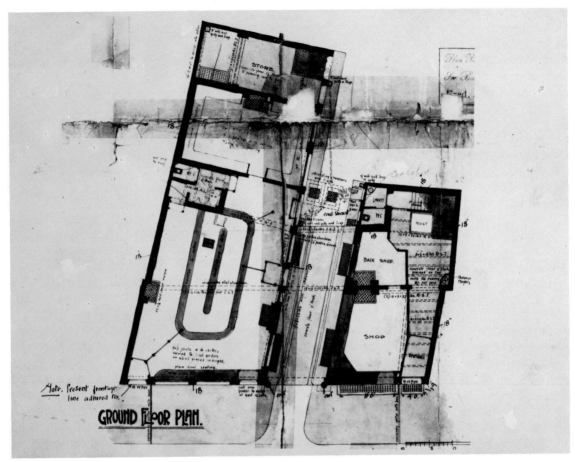

2. Half Moon, 1903 design by B. F. Simpson
(TWA T186/17412)

building's presence on the site since 1550 with an inscription over what is now the main entrance. The Half Moon is one of the pubs mentioned in Mackenzie's 1827 history of Newcastle, when it was 'the resort of many respectable farmers on market-days'; a century later its clientele had changed to lunchtime office workers, when the front bar was slightly reduced in size and the sitting room turned into a luncheon buffet. Arrols still owned the pub at that time but were taken over by the Burton brewers

Samuel Allsopp & Sons Ltd. in 1930. By this means Allsopps obtained a holding of tied houses in Scotland and the north of England. They merged with Ind Coope, originating in Essex but with a brewery in Burton, in 1934 and this combination increased its national market penetration by buying up free houses whenever possible, and by reciprocal trading agreements, whereby two brewers arranged to sell each other's beer. The final step into the national market was taken in 1961 when Ind Coope became part of Allied Breweries with access to pubs throughout Britain.

FREEMANS – THE VINE INN
1 Bigg Market

Opposite the Half Moon on the far side of Bigg Market is Freemans, the site of the Vine Inn until its conversion in 1954. Although the upper facade of the building remains almost unchanged from its days as a pub, all the original interior has gone, a pity as the design of its five bars rivalled Simpson's work in quality and quantity of decorative detail. The Vine was the work of the Oswald architectural practice, founded by Septimus Oswald in 1855. This Newcastle practice designed pubs throughout the north-east and further afield from the mid-nineteenth century until it ceased to function in 1969, and is so important to the history of north-eastern pub design that a later chapter is devoted to its work. The appearance of the Vine today is not due to the Oswalds, however, but to an 1885 rebuilding planned by Arthur Gibson, a local architect. He designed a striking Queen Anne revival elevation in white brick with red window surrounds, capping it with three ball finials. As built, the facade was slightly simplified - no ball finials, gables minus their open topped pediments - and a pale red brick was substituted for the white, resulting in less contrast with the dark red window surrounds. The owners in 1885 were a firm of solicitors, possibly unwilling to invest too much money in a pub which at that time had an unexciting interior, one large bar with a snug leading off.

By 1901 the pub had changed hands and acquired a new licensee, the wine and spirit merchants Bell & Taylor who ran their business from the Bigg Market. They clearly saw the Vine as a showplace for their company, calling in Joseph Oswald & Son to redesign the front bars in

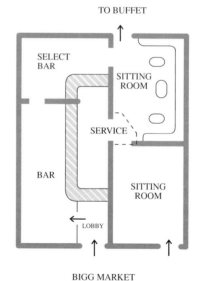

5. Vine, 1901 design by Joseph Oswald & Son; (from TWA 234/3655)

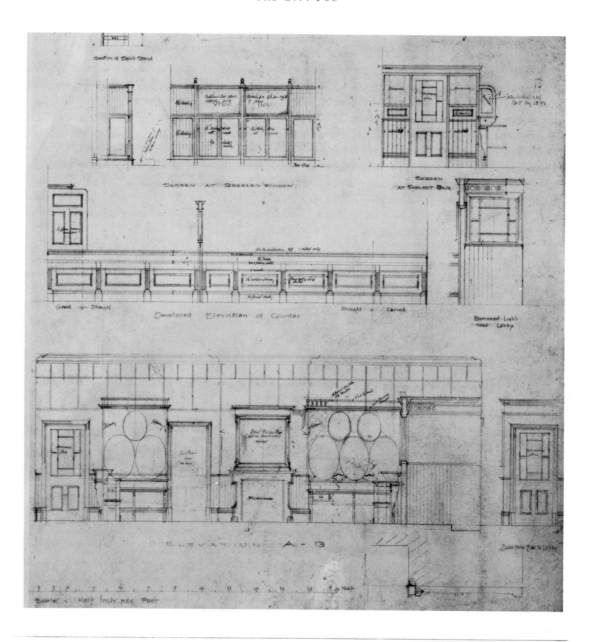

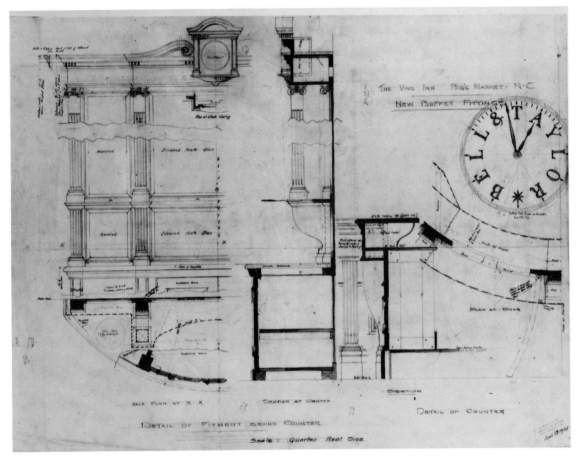

3. *Previous page: Vine, details of 1901 bar fittings by*
Joseph Oswald & Son (TWA 234/3655)
4. *Vine, details of 1908 buffet fittings by*
Joseph Oswald & Son (TWA 234/3650)

December 1901 and the rear buffet in April 1908. Although the plan of the front bar counters is less complex than some of Simpson's designs (see Fig. 5), the detailed joinery of the counter and the back fitting of the bar show late Victorian/Edwardian pub design at its best (see Plate 3). The buffet, fronting on to Pudding Chare, had even more carved pitchpine and decorated glass, as well as a semi-circular bar, a coffered ceiling and a back bar fitting featuring fluted ionic pilasters topped with a clock in which the numerals were replaced with the licensee's name (see Plate 4). All this remained, with few changes apart from an occasional renaming of one of the bars, until 1954 when both front bar and buffet were demolished and a shop installed. The pub had never been in the hands of any of the larger drink companies, and its Edwardian woodwork was doubtless seen as a lost cause by 1954. The quality of its interior showed to perfection the importance of the wine and spirit merchants as pub licensees and owners in Newcastle.

THE BEE HIVE
50 Cloth Market

The Bee Hive was known as a public house in the eighteenth century, being mentioned in the first Newcastle directory of 1778 when its landlord was Cuthbert Burrell. It is a listed grade II building standing on the corner of Cloth Market and High Bridge, important not for any eighteenth century work but for its rebuilding in 1902 by the Oswald practice which designed its present facade (see Plate 5). Its ownership in late Victorian times followed the typical Newcastle pattern, the

5. Bee Hive

North Shields brewers Bartleman and Crighton being in possession as early as 1872, then selling the pub and moving into the Duke of Wellington, further down High Bridge. The freehold went outside the drink trade until 1887 when local brewer James Routledge took over. Routledge never owned many pubs, having only two in Newcastle in 1892, and was taken over by Newcastle Breweries in 1896. The freehold of the Bee Hive passed to Northern Breweries Corporation Ltd., a sister company of Newcastle Breweries which owned a few pubs where development was taking place. The Corporation leased the pub back to Newcastle Breweries who proceeded to rebuild it in 1902.

On such a restricted corner site it was impossible to expand the bar space, which stayed much as it had been under Routledge's ownership with front and rear bars separated by a partial screen and served by one long bar counter. Oswald changed the shape of the counter, making it curve around the new back fitting from the select bar into the small front bar, which was reduced in size to accommodate the entrance to Bee Hive Chambers above the pub. The interior was fitted out almost as originally designed with the exception of the front bar, which was enlarged at the expense of the select bar, the bar counter being made into two adjacent curves (see Fig. 6). The new interior was more decorative and more exclusive than the old, with no direct route between front and select bars, and fortunately the back fitting of the bar remains with its carved ionic columns echoing the design of the window mullions.

The most attractive feature of the exterior of the pub is its ground floor facing of green and yellow faience, a generic term encompassing a variety of special clay mixtures fired at higher temperatures than normal brick (see Plate 6, and Chapter 10 for more on pubs with this type of decoration). The slabs of faience were not shown in detail on Oswald's plans, as they would have been specified at a later stage using ceramic manufacturers' catalogues. The three storeys of office accommodation above the pub had a red brick facade with ashlar dressings, the whole being topped by an ogee tower. The corner site was ideal for a pub as it could attract passing trade from two streets, but in order to do this it had to be noticeable. The combination of the tower, making the pub stand out from a distance, and the coloured glazed faience on the ground floor, differentiating the building from nearby shops and offices, was very effective; architecturally, visually,

the Bee Hive was obviously a pub. The architect also capitalised on the site by carving away the corner of the building where Cloth Market and High Bridge met, the corner door then giving glimpses of the enticing, glittering interior to passers-by taking the shortest route around the corner. Newcastle has, and had, fewer of these 'tile and terracotta' or faience pubs than, for example, Birmingham where the style was very popular in the years 1896-1904. Tyneside pubs in similar style tended to be the product of the early years of the twentieth century, and although they shared the use of corner sites with the

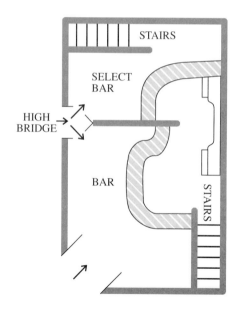

CLOTH MARKET

6. *Bee Hive, built version of 1902 design by Joseph Oswald & Son; (from TWA T186/20141)*

6. Above: *Bee Hive, faience work*
7. Right: *Balmbras*

Birmingham examples, the Tyneside faience pubs used brighter colours; glazed faience in a wide variety of colours rather than unglazed terracotta in shades of red and brown. The principle, however, was the same: the use of design and materials to attract customers.

THE PUBS AROUND THE FOUNTAIN

Ironically given the high density of pubs in the area, the drinking fountain in the middle of Bigg Market, almost at the junction with Cloth and Groat Markets, was built by the Band of Hope Union, a temperance organisation founded in Leeds in 1847. Constructed in 1894, the badly eroded red sandstone memorial bears the maxim 'Water is best', not a view shared by the customers of the 16 pubs in the Market streets at that time. Cloth Market alone had eight pubs, one for every three buildings along its length, and five of these survive today: the Wheat Sheaf (now Balmbra's), The Old Durham House (now Presidents), the Imperial Hotel (now Bewicks), the Old George and the Bee Hive. Balmbra's, after licensee John Balmbra, is one of the most famous pubs in Britain because of its mention in the song 'The Blaydon Races', first performed at the pub's music hall in 1862. The music hall began in 1848, and Balmbra made it the only consistently successful hall in Newcastle; it was the best known in the country outside London. By the turn of the century the pub was part of the Grainger estate, and was rebuilt in 1902 to give the present three storey facade with its pedimented gable (see Plate 7). The gently curving front window contained a window seat, and the curve of the window was repeated in the shape of the bar counter before it straightened

out and ran back to the rear of the public bar. The long, narrow-fronted medieval plots of the Cloth Market precluded any attempt at a complex bar plan by the architect, Stockwell of Pilgrim Street. With the rebuilding came a change of name, from Wheat Sheaf to Carlton Hotel, and tenancy, as the Edinburgh brewers Steel, Coulson & Co. Ltd. took over. Alterations in 1955 saw the bar counter disappear, and the pub was used as a billiard hall before the reintroduction of music hall in 1962, when it became Balmbra's.

Progressing up the Cloth Market towards Bigg Market, in 1894 the next pub would have been the White Hart, taken over two years earlier by John Fitzgerald, the wine and spirit merchant who was just beginning to build up his large holding of public houses. He only owned two in 1892, but was in control of 11 in Newcastle by 1897 and the company he began is the last remaining wine and spirit company to own a chain of pubs on Tyneside. The pub was modernised in 1900 by local architect James Cackett who is rather more interesting than the alterations, which consisted of lengthening the bar in the long, narrow pub. Cackett's partner was Burns Dick, and together they produced Newcastle's Laing Art Gallery and Whitley Bay's domed Spanish City pleasure gardens. The White Hart has disappeared but the Old Durham House (Presidents) still remains. It was separated from the White Hart by only an alleyway, and was another typical Cloth Market pub on a constricted site. In the early 1880s Castle Eden brewer John Nimmo & Sons owned the pub, but by 1894 Bourgogne & Co. (wine and spirit merchants) were tenants and were improving the pub. It was bought by Bass, Ratcliff & Gretton in 1907 as part of their expanding tied house empire.

8. Imperial Hotel

Another alleyway separated the Old Durham House from the Imperial Hotel (Bewicks), a single bar pub on the same pattern as the previous two. Its facade (see Plate 8) dates from a 1909 modernisation, the date being shown above the ground floor window, but from the interior only a few cornice details remain. Recent development has overtaken the sites of the Old White Swan and the Nags Head, the former being a single bar pub owned by the Robinson family of wine and spirit merchants, whose headquarters were at the Nags Head, again a long bar pub. The Old George, standing in Old George Yard behind the 1870 Cloth Market Buildings, is now a grade II listed building with its basis in an early seventeenth century (or possibly older) house. It has undergone many alterations since its days as a coaching inn, including some by Lawson of the Simpson, Lawson and Rayne practice in 1928 when it was owned by George Hogg & Co., Newcastle wine and spirit merchants.

The street and plot pattern of the Cloth Market proved very restrictive for turn of the century pub improvement plans, but this was less of a problem on the other side of the Town Hall in the Groat Market. Near the Cathedral, the Black Boy (now the Blackie Boy and briefly the Coffy Johney) in its original form was associated with Thomas Bewick, who was a member of Swarley's Club, a debating club which met there in the late eighteenth century when it was one of Newcastle's principal inns. Its 1889 rebuilding resulted from the collapse of the back bar, which was standing in ruins when plans for the new pub were submitted in September 1889. The pub was to have a single long bar, although it curved in towards the back fitting near the rear of the bar, giving more space to the back bar; a luncheon bar was screened

Bass of Burton had entered the tied house business at the relatively late date of 1888 when it was floated as a public company, having relied before on the prestige and quality of its beers to maintain sales. By 1900 the company held about 550 houses throughout England and Wales.

off at the far end of the pub. Soon after modernisation the tenancy was taken over by the Emmerson family, local brewers and wine and spirit merchants, and by the time of its next facelift in 1927 was owned by W. B. Reid & Co. Ltd. Ever since its incorporation in 1891 W. B. Reid had been one of Newcastle's major public house owners, second only to the Grainger estate in 1892 with 30 houses, and owning 154 in their entire sales area by the time of their takeover by William Younger in 1956. The 1927 work left the interior unchanged and produced a very plain elevation, the only decoration being raised panels between the windows of the upper floors, still visible today. The interior has since been completely renewed, but some interesting and colourful thirties-style stained glass can be seen in the upper floors of the pub facing Black Boy Yard.

 The pub between the Black Boy and the Lord Chancellor has now disappeared under Thomson House, but the White Horse was well known for its three dimensional sign, a white horse facing out into Groat Market. It was a small pub, with a front bar and a rear sitting room, and had been owned by local brewer Joseph Simpson Arnison throughout the 1870s and 1880s before passing into non-brewer hands until 1909, when Arrols then Vaux of Sunderland leased it. The front bar had a simple half-rectangular bar counter, but this was changed in 1929 to a semi-octagonal counter attached to the back corner of the bar. More alterations in 1933 by the new owners, Newcastle Breweries, simplified the lay-out again. Change of ownership or tenancy usually resulted in rebuilding or, at the least, internal alterations as the new landlord tried to marry the image of the pub with the image of the product being sold. The outcome in design terms was a combination of current architectural trends and fashions in interior design with the brewer's or tenant's view of their product and their clientele. In the case of the White Horse, 1930s streamlined styles plus Newcastle Breweries preference for simple, straightforward design resulted in a plain interior. As in many pubs, the interior had changed from a simple bar into something more complex and back again, this process often taking about 40 years, between the early 1890s boom in High Victorian alterations and the late 1920s.

7. *Earl Grey, 1889 design by Stout & Dockwray; (from TWA T186/13319)*

The pubs in the Bigg Market had most room for expansion of those in the Market streets, and the Half Moon and the Vine took full advantage to produce some spectacular designs. Of the other three pubs on Bigg Market in 1894, the Wheat Sheaf Inn, situated down the narrow passage beside the Half Moon, only lasted another two years before being demolished to make way for new building. It lay behind a watchmaker's shop on Bigg Market and was a simple long bar pub owned by a non-brewer. It had been modernised in 1882 to make four separate drinking areas, including one tiny private bar. The Wheat Sheaf looked out on to Farrington's Court, on the far side of which was the Plough or Old Plough Inn, owned in the 1890s by the Harbottle family, tea dealers. The pub was leased to James Deuchar who controlled half a dozen other pubs in Newcastle by 1894. Across the road at 7 Bigg Market lay the Earl Grey Inn, a pub with bars on two floors owned by Simpson the brewer until 1889, when it was bought by L. Pearson & Co., boot manufacturers who ran the shop next door. As to be expected on change of ownership they immediately modernised the pub, making a corner snug in the front bar and introducing a grill room at the rear (see Fig. 7). Upstairs were two select rooms, one each for ladies and gentlemen, and a sitting room. Emmersons took over the tenancy in 1892, but in 1900 the licence was allowed to lapse, the pub and the coffee palace next door probably making way for new development.

The pubs of the Market streets at the end of the nineteenth century show the importance of style in the beer sales war. The large pubs in particular were altered again and again to keep up with changing drinking habits and markets, giving scope to some excellent architects to dazzle with decoration in a manner impossible in more sedate buildings. Their work has continued to make an impact on the appearance of central Newcastle although many of their finest interiors have been transformed, often now to a pastiche of the High Victorian style of the originals. The city centre pubs were profitable, thus owners and tenants could afford to invest money in visually attractive facades and complex interiors; in the suburbs, the relationship between architecture and the customer was often rather different.

CHAPTER TWO

The Ouseburn Trail

from Byker to Gosforth

THE Ouse Burn is a small river which flows south along Newcastle's eastern edge to join the Tyne near Byker, but to walk along its banks is to see tremendous contrasts in landscape, buildings and industry. The Metro traveller has a splendid panoramic view of the mouth of the Ouse Burn when crossing the viaduct on the journey between Byker and the city centre, and Byker Metro Station makes a convenient starting place for walking the Ouseburn Trail with its twelve pubs.

If you start from the Metro Station, leave on the north side and turn left along Corbridge Street, walking down to the roundabout where the Metro viaduct crosses the road and you find the first pub, the Plough, nestling against the Byker Wall (see Fig. 8). In the twenty years between 1885 and 1905 it was gradually altered, changing from a simple two bar pub into a sophisticated six room establishment catering for the local population who lived in the surrounding terrace houses and worked in the highly industrial area at the mouth of the Ouse Burn. In 1885 its appearance was that of a pair of terraced

houses, the bar and snug being side by side along the frontage. In that year its owner, Roger Watson, brought in a local contractor to change the facade into more of a shop front, with large windows and three doors leading to a single front room with a long bar. The Plough was bought by Robert Deuchar before 1896 and assumed the rather incongruous identity of Ye Olde Plough Inn, probably when Deuchar made internal alterations around the turn of the century. Both the front bar and the back of the pub, originally private, were transformed on an unusual six bar plan which kept the counter but changed almost everything around it (see Fig. 9). Deuchar thus obtained four bars and two bottle and jug rooms for the take-out trade. The pub remained basically the same even after 1905, when Deuchar slightly altered one of the back bars.

Turn down Byker Bank, leaving the Plough on your left, and almost immediately follow Byker Buildings along to your right as far as the Cumberland Arms, looking out over the Ouse Burn. At the turn of the century the view would have been

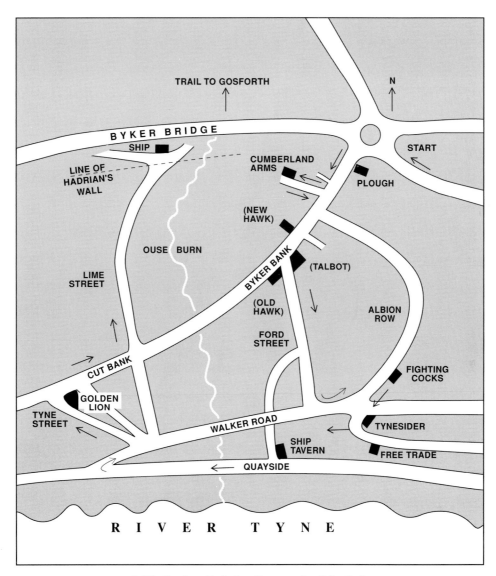

8. *The Ouseburn Trail, Ouse Burn mouth to Byker Bridge*

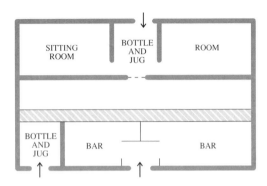

9. The Plough at the end of the nineteenth century; (from TWA T186/21436)

partly obscured by rows of terraced houses dropping down into the valley, as well as the smoke and dust of heavy industry. Within this small area at the mouth of the Burn lay two lead works, glass, canvas and iron works and two potteries, as well as a sweet factory and the cattle sanatorium. Some of the factory and warehouse buildings remain, and are being converted for office and light industrial use; the Cluny whisky warehouse, just south of Byker City Farm (once a lead works!), is currently being restored. Heavy industry meant a high density of pubs for thirsty workers. In 1896, within about two hundred yards of the Byker Bank crossing of the Ouse Burn were eleven pubs, only one of which still stands today, and significantly its use has changed to a windsurfing centre.

The Cumberland Arms as it appears today is the result of a rebuilding in 1898-99 (see Plate 9). It might have been a very different pub, as can be seen from Benjamin Simpson's suggested design for the site dating from January 1898 (see Plate 10). Simpson had drawn up plans for the owner, one Mr

Thompson of Whickham, and had produced a dramatic three storey building complete with corner tower, ideal for a city centre site but out of place in Byker's terraces. Thompson turned down the plan, although it had the approval of the Town Improvement Committee, probably for commercial rather than aesthetic reasons as Simpson had enlarged the pub to take in two back-to-back cottages also on the site. Thompson would have lost the rent from the cottages as well as having to find the cost of a total rebuilding. He turned instead to the equally well known James Cackett, who merely proposed a few internal alterations to increase the bar area, and a new facade with some decorative

9. Cumberland Arms

W. GEO. LAWS. *Town Surveyor*

—— FRONT ELEVATION. ——

10. *Cumberland Arms, 1898 design by*
B. F. Simpson, not built (TWA T186/17868)

touches, leaving the cottages alone. Although Simpson's interior with its enlarged bar and two sitting rooms remains but a set of drawings, Cackett's interior has fortunately survived largely unchanged. He retained the basic plan of the pub with bar and sitting room side by side along the main front, but added a new back bar fitting which dominates the left hand bar, and belies the plain exterior.

Return to Byker Bank and walk down towards the Ouse Burn, turning left along Ford Street. On this corner at the turn of the century two pubs faced each other, the Talbot Hotel and, on the lower side, the Old Hawk Inn (the New Hawk Inn was just across Byker Bank). The Old Hawk was a small pub with a front bar and a back tap room, leased by Arrols in 1905. The tenant only took about £10 a week, although Arrols thought it should be over £15, and the pub had no decent toilet facilities. The Oswald architectural practice were called in to draw up plans to improve and enlarge the pub, but the probable return on any investment was not high, and the unimproved pub lost its wine and spirit licence in 1905, reverting to a beerhouse.

Follow Ford Street down to its meeting with Walker Road and bear left into Albion Row; across the road is the Fighting Cocks, known in the early 1980s as Ye Olde Fighting Cocks. Before its 1897 rebuilding the Fighting Cocks was a two storey brick building on a stone plinth, its two bars placed either side of a central door. This was a common plan for

11. Fighting Cocks

smaller, out-of-town pubs, which retained an area of private accommodation for the landlord in the rear of the building. In 1897 Arthur Stockwell was asked to redesign the Fighting Cocks by its owners Reid & Co. The present facade with its twin decorative gables is almost unchanged from his original plans, although the interior has been completely modernised (see Plate 11). Stockwell's interior comprised four main rooms with a small bottle and jug, all served from a central semi-rectangular bar counter (see Fig. 10). As with Simpson's rejected plan for the Cumberland Arms, the design could be mistaken for that of a city centre pub, and would have caught the eye of the traveller on the riverside road to Walker.

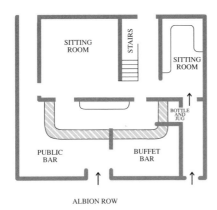

ALBION ROW

10. Fighting Cocks, 1897 design by Arthur Stockwell; (from TWA T186/17553)

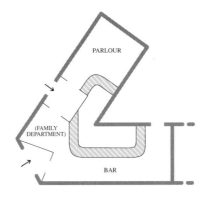

11. Free Trade Inn, 1895 design by Septimus Oswald & Son and alterations to 1911; (from TWA T186/16526)

Directly across Walker Road from the Fighting Cocks is the now disused Tynesider, a small street corner pub originally named the Rose and Crown. Just beyond it on St Lawrence Road is the Free Trade Inn, an inconspicuous pub but another case of ambitious design thwarted by lack of finance. In 1895 the pub was owned by Henry Davidson, owner of four pubs in Newcastle in 1892. Davidson decided to rebuild in 1895, and Oswald & Son suggested a design in which the tenant's accommodation would have been severely restricted by the amount of space given over to the bar and club room. The suggested elevation on the basically V-shaped site had two large, decorative gables in Queen Anne revival style with ball finials, and a hooded canopy over the door. Inside, the single room bar had a V-shaped counter, the club room being on the first floor. These plans were withdrawn and replaced six months later by a version which increased the size of the tenant's kitchen and living room, and replaced the club room

with bedrooms. Davidson went ahead with the latter design, probably because it combined lower cost with higher income from the tenant. The facade had hardly any decoration except facings round the windows and a parapet inscribed with the name of the pub (the lettering can still just be distinguished).

By 1911, when the pub had been sold to South Shields brewers Matthew Wood & Son, the tenant's kitchen had made way for a parlour, the bar counter being extended round to the rear of the pub, and the family department had become part of the main bar after removal of a partition (see Fig. 11). More internal partitions had been removed by 1937, when Newcastle Breweries were in charge of the pub, having taken over Matthew Wood in 1919, and the current bar consists of three loosely differentiated areas which were previously the bar and the tenant's kitchen and living room. There is little left of the original interior except the basic form of the bar counter and part of the back bar fitting, although it is possible to judge the positions of the partitions by studying the internal decoration.

From the Free Trade Inn, turn back a few yards and take the steps down to Maling Street, where the Ship Tavern stands almost at the mouth of the Ouse Burn. The design of the pub is an interesting combination of black and white half timbering on the first floor with a lightly classical ground floor, combining red brick and fluted pilasters in fawn faience (see Plate 12). From the Quayside in front of the pub there is an expansive view along the river Tyne. Cross the Ouse Burn and walk along Quayside towards the city, taking a sharp right turn up Horatio Street. At the top of the street is a drinking trough and statue of William Coulson (1841-1911), secretary of the Northumberland Association for the Protection of Women and Children, erected by public subscription in memory of his work for humans and animals.

Turn left up Tyne Street to its junction with City Road, where you will find the Golden Lion, now a windsurfing shop but once a three storey street corner pub. In 1891 it was owned by J. Duncan & Co. who commissioned Benjamin Simpson to modernise its single bar, which at that time took up most of the ground floor. Simpson produced a relatively simple plan which created four bars by using screens and including the landlord's previously private sitting room in the public area; the bar

12. Ship Tavern

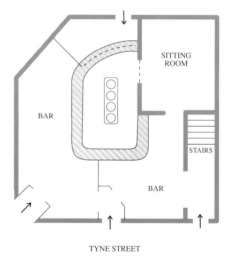

12. Golden Lion, 1891 design by B. F. Simpson; (from TWA T186/ 14283)

13. Ship

counter filled the centre of the ground floor (see Fig. 12). Although the plan was straightforward, the introduction of small bar areas at the early date of 1891 was unusual. The ground plan remained much the same until the 1950s, except for some tinkering with partitions which resulted in the two main bars becoming one. The change of use from pub to shop means that another Simpson interior has been demolished, and in this case the exterior was unremarkable.

Turn right along Cut Bank and walk almost down to the Ouse Burn. The Royal Sovereign, Mason's Arms, Blue Bell and Plumbers Arms, present on Cut Bank in 1896, have all disappeared. Turn left at Lime Street, walking parallel to the Burn and across the route of Hadrian's Wall to the Ship Inn, next to the City Farm. The three storey brick built Ship stood in the middle of a terrace of eight or nine buildings at the turn of the century, but is now the sole remnant of the terrace with a dramatic site almost under the arches of the Byker Road bridge (see Plate 13).

Walk either side of the pub and take the path leading under the arches of the road, Metro and rail bridges to the point at which the Ouse Burn ceases to be tidal and runs into a culvert. The path continues up and over a recreation ground, once another lead works, to Warwick Street. Cross over to Newington Road and go immediately right down Stratford Grove West to rejoin the Burn as it reappears in Jesmond Vale. Here the scenery changes from industrial to arcadian, and many paths can be taken through Heaton Park, Armstrong Park and Jesmond Dene to Gosforth (about two miles). Following the course of the Ouse Burn, look out for the Blue Bell on the far side of the first road crossing, in Spring Bank Road. The nineteenth century Blue Bell Inn was owned by Robert Deuchar and was a five room pub with a single bar counter; in effect, the pub had one bar and four sitting rooms. Deuchar tried to modernise the pub in 1887 by combining the bar with two sitting rooms and enlarging the counter, but permission was refused because of worries about the siting of new drains. Between the pub and the Burn was the pub's walled garden, just above the mill race for the flint mill which stood slightly downstream.

Head roughly north through Heaton Park into Armstrong Park, presented to the city by armament maker Lord Armstrong in 1880. Cross Benton Bank by the bridge connecting the park with Jesmond Dene, at the eastern end of the Armstrong Bridge across the Ouse Burn, opened 1878. The Dene was also a gift to the city from Armstrong, and was formally opened to the public in 1884. Leave the Dene at Castles Farm Road just north of the racquet court, a red brick building with an imposing circular window overlooking the valley. Turn left, and then right at Matthew Bank and continue into Haddricksmill Road, where the Millstone occupies the site of the old Mill Inn and the attached soda water factory.

The new Millstone was built in 1898 for J. H. Graham using plans drawn up by James Cackett, the exterior remaining today very much as it was originally designed in red brick with stone dressings (see Plate 14). Its main feature was the decorative

14. Millstone

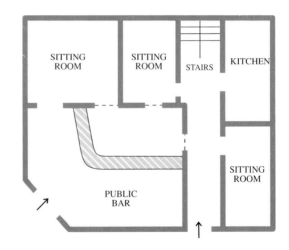

13. Millstone, 1898 design by James Cackett; (from TWA 251/11 no 678)

15. Brandling Villa

gable facing the main road, which has lost its pair of ball finials and had a window inserted in place of a niche. Cackett's interior used a single bar counter in the public bar to serve three sitting rooms by means of hatches (see Fig. 13); there was also a billiard or club room on the first floor.

Further along Haddricksmill Road at the roundabout lies the Brandling Villa, built in 1900 for W. B. Reid & Co. and designed by Arthur Stockwell, the same combination which produced the Fighting Cocks (see Plate 15). The pub previously on the site was a two storey stone building with its tap room and public bar to left and right of a central door, but the new Villa was much larger, a hotel as well as a pub. The sandstone exterior is reminiscent of a small scale baroque town hall, with its balcony and decorative

finials and gablets; it has survived much as originally planned, as is shown by a drawing of the pub made in 1912, eleven years after its opening (see Plate 16). Stockwell's interior was split between pub and hotel usage, the pub consisting of a large public bar which served two sitting rooms and a bottle and jug (see Fig. 14). He seemed to reserve his decorative flourishes for the exterior, unlike Simpson and the Oswald practice.

Across the roundabout from the Villla to Killingworth Road, and victory is in sight, the end of the Ouseburn Trail! More precisely, the Victory, a small pub which has stood on the site since at least the middle of the nineteenth century. The Ouse Burn itself flows north west through Gosforth Golf Course, with no further pubs in its vicinity. To finish

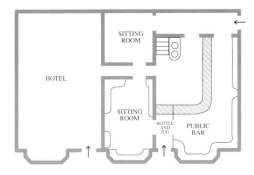

HADDRICKSMILL ROAD

14. Brandling Villa, Haddricksmill Road, South Gosforth, 1900 design by Arthur Stockwell (Tyne & Wear Archives Service)

the trail at the nearest Metro station, turn right from the Victory up Station Road to South Gosforth Station.

The trail runs from a heavy industrial site to the edge of rural Northumberland, taking in pubs which vary from the small local to the large hotel. The most prominent change to the Ouseburn Trail pubs over the last century has been the modernisation and enlargement of the twin bar front pubs, turning them into less decorative, less complex versions of city pubs. The same band of well known architects worked for the same brewers as in the city centre, but their designs were smaller and simpler; away from the centre, pubs did not need to advertise themselves on such a grand scale. Many pubs along the route of the trail have been demolished or have changed their use, but those which remain have grown from their terraced house origins to examples of plain, but not uninteresting, turn of the century everyday pub design.

16. Left: Brandling Villa Haddricksmill Road, South Gosforth, in August 1912, drawn by J.F. Conn (Tyne & Wear Archives Service)

CHAPTER THREE

At the Quayside

North Shields

TO approach the New Quay at North Shields by the Tyne ferry is to see the Market Place almost as the Duke of Northumberland intended it in the early years of the nineteenth century, the Northumberland Arms dominating the quayside buildings. The New Quay was laid out about 1770, and the Duke of Northumberland's Surveyor and Architect David Stephenson designed the Market Place buildings which were erected between 1806 and 1817. Stephenson, a Newcastle man, is best known for his exquisite All Saints Church near the Tyne Bridge, a classical design with baroque overtones on an oval plan (1786-96). The Market Place was never completed, the intention being to enclose all three sides of the New Quay with four storey classical buildings, this imposing image being presented in a watercolour of 1810 by John Dobson, who was then a young apprentice in the Stephenson practice. The design for the Market Place is similar in concept to the classical rebuilding taking place in Edinburgh at the end of the eighteenth century, but all that remains is 13 bays of the original 21 bay section on

the west of the quayside, opposite the river. The Northumberland Arms was the centrepiece of the range, but the southernmost eight bays have been demolished, giving a lop-sided effect.

Instead of being surrounded by tall classical buildings, the quayside is overlooked by an interesting variety of pubs. The Porthole on the north side is the work of W. & T. R. Milburn of Sunderland, designers of ornate theatres in Sunderland and South Shields. Facing it to the south is the Chain Locker, a product of the Oswald practice but not of its decorative late Victorian period. Although the New Quay area was thick with pubs at the end of the nineteenth century, the decline of the quayside has seen most of them demolished. A reminder of the past can just be seen through the Smiths Shiprepairers dock gates, where high above the quay to the south stands the Wolsington House, a giant pub built in 1902 for the Tynemouth innkeeper A. N. Dodds to cater for the then expanding port of North Shields. The story of the remaining pubs on and around the New Quay reflects the economic history of the area; the existence of a pub may now be the only visible evidence of previous prosperity.

NORTHUMBERLAND ARMS

David Stephenson was present on 14 October 1806 when the foundation stone of the Market Place buildings was laid, accompanied by a nine gun salute. His Northumberland Arms Hotel is a four storey, five bay sandstone ashlar building of classical design, with a rusticated ground floor and engaged giant ionic columns stretching across the first and second floors (see Plate 17). Topping the facade is a balustrade which originally carried the Duke of Northumberland's coat of arms above its central panel. Just above the pilasters beside the porch are small crescents, symbols of the Percy family.

The listed grade II building has always been a hotel or public house, traditionally known as the 'Jungle'. The newly renovated building adjacent to it was the Sailors' Home, the Market Place being an important meeting point for sailors looking for work.

17. Northumberland Arms

A witness giving evidence in 1853 before the House of Commons Select Committee on Public Houses and Places of Entertainment estimated that North Shields was home to about 300 'women of the town', around one for every hundred of the population. Sailors were said to stay in public houses when ashore, where they found 'facilities not only of spending their money, but of sometimes ruining their health'. At that time there were 217 pubs in the Borough of Tynemouth, which included North Shields as well as Tynemouth and Cullercoats. There was certainly a great concentration of pubs by the river, with 27 listed in 1850 as being present on the New Quay, Clive Street and Duke Street, immediately to the north and south of the Quay. In 1848 the Northumberland Arms was controlled by Bartleman and Crighton, the North Shields brewers, who were looking for a tenant in November of that year.

The Northumberland Arms was taken over in 1897 by R. W. Cummins, and within two years he had redecorated and refurnished the entire hotel, using Newcastle architects Marshall and Dick to redesign the ground floor incorporating new service areas and bars. The planning application was submitted to the Borough of Tynemouth Urban Sanitary Authority and approved in October 1898, and by the following year Cummins was catering for the shipbuilding trade, with public luncheons and dinners, and functions related to steamship trials. The ground floor of the hotel (see Fig. 15) comprised three bars and a small dining room, and on the upper floors were a coffee room, billiard room, smoke rooms and a dining room which could seat about 100 guests. The buffet bar on the south front had a semicircular counter, the north front bar a curving

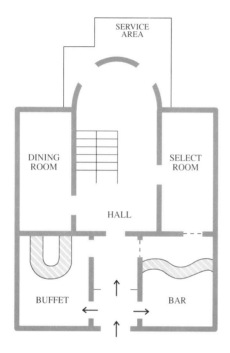

MARKET PLACE

*15. Northumberland Arms in 1898;
(from NTPD)*

*18. The Market Place between the wars
(NSLSC ACC 8302)*

counter, but nothing remains of these late Victorian interiors. To the rear of the hotel were the service area and toilets, built in and around the full height stone bow which Stephenson had designed for the west facade (this is still visible from the car park).

In spite of all his work on the hotel, Cummins sold up within five years of taking over, perhaps showing a profit on his investment. By 1903 the Newcastle wine and spirit merchants A. H. Higginbottom & Co. were in control, keeping the pub until the mid-1920s when brewers Maclay &

Co. Ltd. bought it. Maclay were an Alloa company with an office in Newcastle, a common pre-war arrangement for the many non-local brewers trading on Tyneside. The Northumberland Arms eventually passed to Whitbreads after the war. The view of the Market Place between the wars (see Plate 18) shows the Northumberland Arms facing the busy quayside, with the Golden Fleece, now the Porthole, in the background.

PORTHOLE - GOLDEN FLEECE

The most noticeable alteration to the exterior of the Golden Fleece since it was built in 1897 is the change of name. Its solid red brick and terracotta has hardly weathered, and even one of the two original golden fleece carvings on the doorcases has survived to give away the identity of the pub. A pub was on the site in 1850, when the landlord was Thomas Robson, succeeded in the mid-1850s by the Brown family, who held the pub for around 25 years. James

Deuchar took over the pub before the turn of the century, expanding from his Newcastle base where in 1892 he had held eight pubs. Deuchar used the Sunderland firm of W. and T. R. Milburn to produce a design for rebuilding the pub in August 1897, the Golden Fleece then having a single long bar counter which, by a complex system of corridors and hatches, served five small sitting rooms and a bar. The Milburn practice were at that time working on the Empire Music Hall in South Shields, built in 1898-9 under their supervision but designed by theatre specialist Frank Matcham, famous for his tremendously ornate interiors. Its King Street facade has a stepped gable with decorative swags; the experience of working closely on a Matcham building may have influenced the work of the local practice, as the slightly stepped and definitely ornate gables of the Golden Fleece show a common link

with the theatre design. The practice were eclectic architects, in Sunderland building a Methodist Church (1902- 3), the classical Water Company offices (1905-7), the Magistrates Court (1907) and the Empire Theatre (1907), this time entirely and successfully to their own design. They were not often used for pubs on Tyneside, but on such an important site, and with the spectacular competition of the revitalised Northumberland Arms so close, Deuchar probably thought it worthwhile to look for an unusual design.

The Milburns retained the basic long, rectangular shape of the old pub but changed the interior completely, producing a more select portion near the river, with two sitting rooms and a buffet, and an L-shaped bar facing Clive Street (see Fig. 16). The bar was split into three areas by screens, but the plans give no clue as to the interior decoration.

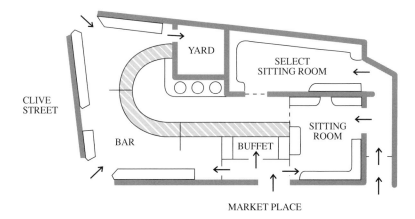

16. Golden Fleece, 1897 design by W. & T. R. Milburn;
(from NTPD)

19. Porthole

The exterior was dominated by two gables, each topped by a sandstone scallop and ball finial (see Plate 19). The easternmost part of the pub was the most decorative, with an oriel window and a semicircular window to the front sitting room. The external decoration, particularly the carved doorcases, emphasised that this part of the pub contained the more select rooms. The Clive Street bar entrances were relatively plain, although overlooked by a ribbed chimney-stack, but between the two gables facing the quay was a first floor balcony which most nearly resembled a theatre box. Rather than an addition to the facade it was formed from an indentation in the south face, and the arch was highlighted by the use of shiny terracotta facings. From here, one could look out over the forum of the quayside, as if in the best seats at the Empire.

Deuchar had found an idiosyncratic design, but one which combined spectacle with efficiency, as the single bar counter was sited so that it could serve all six areas of the pub. The interior has been lost to twentieth century modernisation but neither Deuchar, who was still in control of the pub in 1939, or its later owners have tampered with the exterior, which continues to maintain the identity of the Golden Fleece rather than the Porthole.

OLD BLACK LION

When James Deuchar modernised the Golden Fleece, his closest competition was not from the Northumberland Arms but from the Black Lion, which stood only a few yards to the north, on what is now the North Eastern Rubber factory site. It was a four storey Georgian brick building with a corner entrance and some interesting detailing. The pub curved gently to fit its site, the corner section being slightly recessed, and two circular upper storey windows were dressed with decorative stone facings. It was not a spectacular building, but as the Black Lion or Old Black Lion, had existed on Clive Street since at least 1850 when its landlady was Mary Dawson. None of the large breweries took the pub over before the Second World War and it was still functioning as a pub in 1964, although scheduled for demolition. By 1966 it was about to become a betting shop, and demolition followed shortly afterwards. It was one of the 16 pubs in Clive Street in 1850, stretching alphabetically from the Bay Horse to the Waterloo. As quayside activities decreased in importance during the twentieth century, so the intricate mass of buildings on the river's edge were demolished, with only a few plaques now indicating the presence of old quays. The Old Black Lion, an unreconstructed Georgian building, could not have been a good proposition as a modern pub, and doubtless this contributed to its demolition while rebuilt pubs like the Chain Locker on the south of the New Quay survived.

CHAIN LOCKER–CRANE HOUSE

Today's version of the Chain Locker was rebuilt in 1905, as the plaque above the door tells us, but a pub has stood on the site since at least 1850 when it was known as Crane House, after a dockside crane. Its landlord for over 30 years in the last century was Thomas Walker, who took over the pub before 1865 and left about 1898, by which time Crane House was part of the Newcastle Breweries empire; they owned 28 of the Borough of Tynemouth's 207 pubs in 1892. Only the Duke of Northumberland could compete with them as a local landlord, with 13 pubs in the Borough.

Crane House came into the hands of Newcastle Breweries on the formation of the company in 1890, as it had previously belonged to W. H. Allison & Co. of North Shields, wine and spirit merchants and brewers, one of the constituent parts of the new firm. Allisons brewed at the High Brewery, built in 1871 almost opposite Crane House on the river side of Duke Street (it is now a kittiwake colony!) The pub had been purchased in 1861 on a part freehold, part leasehold basis, and the Newcastle Breweries Register of Mortgages records that by 1890 the deeds had disappeared. It became known as a Swinburne house, another part of Newcastle Breweries, around 1900 and kept that designation until about 1931 when the Swinburne name was replaced by that of Newcastle Breweries.

Plans for rebuilding the pub were submitted in February 1904 by Joseph Oswald & Son for the Breweries, and building work was completed in 1905,

20. *Chain Locker*

leaving the pub much as it is today externally (see Plate 20). The style is reminiscent of the Arts and Crafts architect Norman Shaw with a large oriel window on the east facade, a tall chimney and two prominent gables, although late Victorian pub tradition is maintained in the Edwardian era with a ground floor faced in glazed faience. Fluted ionic pilasters separate the ground floor windows and floral faience panels fill the spandrels, while in the cornice

21. Chain Locker faience work

Street gable, and a flag-pole above the door; the flag-pole was in existence at one time, as its slot can still be seen in the parapet. At ground floor level, the Oswald drawings specified no facings, and differed on window design from the actual building; it seems probable that the faience work was ordered from a manufacturer's catalogue at a later stage in the planning of the new pub.

The new interior was a simple combination of front bar and rear sitting room, served by a single bar counter in the front bar with a hatch to the back room. The original glasswork contained pictures of a dockside crane, but this has disappeared, sold abroad. Nothing remains of the original Oswald interior, but the drawings imply that it may have been less ornate than some of the practice's city pubs. Newcastle Breweries sold the pub after the last war, and it eventually became a free house known as the Chain Locker, the new name board unfortunately obscuring part of the faience work.

Although the pub now stands isolated at the end of the New Quay, in 1900 it was the last building in Duke Street, a narrow passage which led round via the Bull Ring to the rear of the docks to the south, owned by Edwards & Sons. Of the 50 numbered buildings in Duke Street, five were pubs and one was the High Brewery, which continued as a working brewery after 1890 although the main brewery for Newcastle Breweries was the Tyne Brewery in Newcastle. Barrels were transported between the two breweries by a boat named 'The Brewer'. By the end of the First World War most of the buildings on the river side of Duke Street had been demolished or found new uses, the Ferry House and the Essex Arms amongst them. The Turks Head lasted until the 1930s, and was a James Deuchar pub on the Crane

dentil and egg and dart mouldings are combined. The name of the pub was changed to Crane House Vaults during the rebuilding, the 'Vaults' part of the faience still being visible on the north facade (see Plate 21). The original design was rather more ornate, with a ribbed chimney-stack, a small canopy over the door and applied half-timbering on the gables (the latter may be hidden beneath the pebble dash). There was also a small window in the Duke

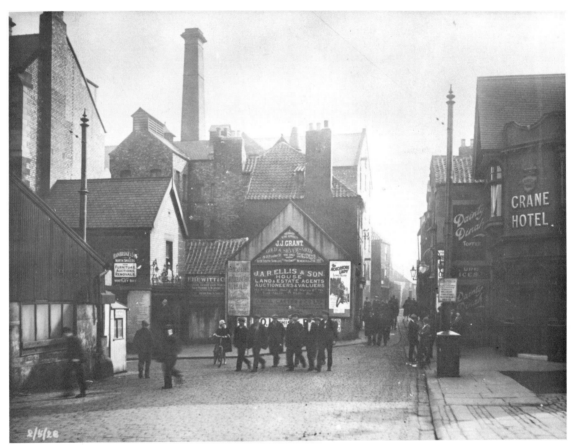

22. Crane House and Duke Street, 2 May 1928 (NSLSC 6506)

House side of Duke Street which was taken over by Swinburne/Newcastle Breweries in the 1920s. The Phoenix Hotel, only seven doors away from Crane House, was still in existence in the mid-1950s and was also a Swinburne/Newcastle Breweries house. Its site was just inside the Smiths dock gates, the view from the gates now an open expanse compared with the tightly packed mass of mainly commercial buildings which formed Duke Street between the wars (see Plate 22). Above the roofs of the Shiprepairers' works can be seen the gable and chimney- stacks of the Wolsington House, looking down on the docks from Burdon Main Row.

PHOENIX

The Phoenix had stood on Duke Street since at least 1850, but was rebuilt in 1902 for Newcastle Breweries to a design by Joseph Oswald & Son. The first design submitted to the planning authority in July 1900 had verged on the classical, with ionic columns on the first floor of what appeared to be a stone facade, the whole topped by a lantern. The pub had a simple plan, a long front bar taking up the entire width of the site, with two sitting rooms at the rear served by hatches from the counter. Although this design was approved, Newcastle Breweries did not build it, instead opting for the inclusion of a shop in the site plan. The revised design was submitted in February 1902, the shop taking space from the front bar but earning a rental for the Brewery from what was a leasehold property. The two back rooms, now called select and sitting rooms, were still served via hatches from the front bar which had taken on an L-shape to

accommodate the shop (see Fig. 17). The elevation had been simplified, perhaps to cut the building costs; the ionic columns and lantern were omitted, the only decorative touches being small panels of floral faience work between the ground floor windows.

Duke Street led past the Phoenix to the Bull Ring and Dotwick Street, at the back of the docks. Changes were taking place to the two Dotwick Street pubs around the turn of the century as brewers and wine and spirit merchants fought for their share of the expanding North Shields trade. The Clarendon Hotel was bought by the Newcastle upon Tyne Wine & Spirit Co. about 1900, while the Bee Hive became an Arrol pub in 1901. It had previously belonged to Dover & Newsome Baxter Ltd., a combination of Newcastle wine and spirit merchants Dover & Co. and North Yorkshire brewers Newsome Baxter, formed in 1897. Arrols took over the Newcastle part of the company in 1901, thus gaining

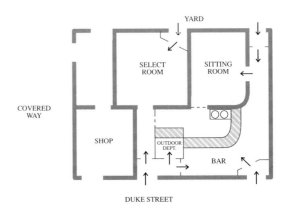

17. Phoenix Hotel, 1902 design by Joseph Oswald & Son; (from NTPD)

more outlets for their products. Also changing hands at this time was the Wolsington House, just around the corner in Burdon Main Row.

WOLSINGTON HOTEL

There has been a licensed house on the site of the Wolsington since at least 1834, when John Veitch's alehouse was mentioned in a directory of North Shields. It became a fully licensed house by the mid-nineteenth century, and was taken over in the early 1870s by William Taylor. Charles William Taylor, probably the son of William, took it on around 1895. The younger Taylor was a North Shields innkeeper, owning three other pubs in the town including the Tynemouth Lodge, still standing on Tynemouth Road. He began to sell his pubs towards the turn of the century, the Wolsington being bought by Andrew Nichol Dodds just before 1900. Dodds was a well known Tynemouth character, an innkeeper, philanthropist and local councillor who had begun working life as a blacksmith. He was born in Jesmond in 1830 and became a political radical, a Chartist and pioneer of the local co-operative movement. He also bred Bedlington Terriers and homing pigeons, winning shows with his dogs. At the age of 30 he changed from blacksmith to publican, moving to North Shields where he rapidly built up a profitable chain of pubs; in 1892 he owned five in the Borough of Tynemouth and two in South Shields.

Dodds decided to rebuild the Wolsington immediately he bought it, the first set of plans being submitted in August 1900 by John Spencer, a North Shields architect. Spencer's Wolsington House Hotel was centred on a bar counter in the form of an almost complete rectangle from which four main rooms were served: two sitting rooms, a buffet and the public bar. Although these plans were approved by the Sanitary Authority, Dodds did not go ahead with building, possibly because the design was inefficient, devoting too great a part of the floor area to corridors between various rooms. The corridors took up space which could have been in the money-earning bar area. Spencer's second attempt, dated 17 May 1901, retained the central bar counter and four public rooms, but was a more sophisticated design. It was also aimed at a different market, with the two sitting rooms replaced by a dining room and a 'smoke and news room' (see Fig. 18). The elevation was much the same in both versions of the plans: a tall, two storey red brick building with a wooden corner tower and decorative shaped and dutch gables. The Wolsington was built in 1902 much as it was designed, the most striking feature of the elevation being the gable facing the river, which not only has a pediment topped with a giant fleur-de-lis but a large circular terracotta plaque set just below it (see Col. Plate 1). The stiff-leaf carving on the sandstone dressings has weathered very badly. The basic structure of the interior still remains, as do some of the original bar fittings in the double height front bar, notably the bar counter itself.

A. N. Dodds died in August 1904, leaving the pub to one of his two sons, John, who kept it until just after the First World War when it was taken over by W. B. Reid & Co.

The pubs of the New Quay area are a very mixed bunch architecturally, ranging from the listed Georgian Northumberland Arms to the Edwardian Arts and Crafts inspired Crane House. Many of them underwent a change of ownership or rebuilding,

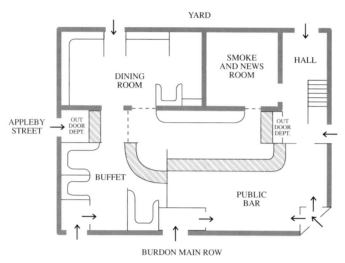

18. Wolsington House, 1901 design by John Spencer;
(from NTPD)

often both, in the few years around the turn of the century when North Shields was expanding from its industrial origins to become a major fishing port. 76 steam trawlers, a North Shields innovation, were based there in 1909 with many more visiting, and the fishing trade then employed around 2600 people, rising to nearly 6000 at the height of the herring season when 600 herring boats used the port. Clearly this was an important market for the brewers, particularly in view of the increased competition in the brewing industry at the turn of the century. The new owners of the quayside pubs tried, as usual, to entice customers inside by providing splendid or exotic buildings, obviously different from the surrounding commercial architecture. Some architectural practices regarded pub work as a staple, but for others it was a rarity, and perhaps a chance to

experiment with new styles and decorative forms which would be appropriate to buildings dedicated to entertainment as well as commerce. The Wolsington and the Porthole come from practices not well known for their public house work, but both are fine examples of turn of the century idiosyncrasy in pub style. They are not listed buildings, and perhaps do not deserve to be as individual buildings on purely architectural grounds, but if these and other similar pubs were ever to be demolished, an entire strand of Victorian/Edwardian design would disappear. The pubs were generally not grand, classical buildings but were fun architecture with a serious commercial purpose, and are certainly an important part of architectural and social history.

CHAPTER FOUR

Beside the Seaside

Tynemouth

TYNEMOUTH has been a seaside resort since the late eighteenth century, when the presence of the military garrison at Tynemouth Castle acted as an attraction for polite society. It was then a small village, consisting of a few terraces and squares of houses, and remained so until the middle of the following century when the railway came. Its popularity as a resort had declined by the 1830s, when it was described in uninviting terms by a visitor:

'I never saw anything less inviting, or more discouraging for a bather...than the appearance of every thing around. Towards the cliffs a few mean-looking houses are let as lodgings during the season; but there is a great dearth of house accommodation at that period.' The Bath Hotel (now the Royal Sovereign) dates from the resort's initial period of growth, but Tynemouth's main period of expansion came in the 1870s when 720,000 people a year visited the resort and the great crescent of Percy Gardens was built.

In 1882 Tynemouth Station, the town's first through station, was opened. This extravagant iron and glass structure was designed by William Bell, architect to the North Eastern Railway from 1877 to 1923, who was a specialist in intricate iron platform awnings. The Victorian resort's attractions included the Winter Garden, the Crystal Palace of the North, perched on the cliffs above Long Sands. It opened in 1878, but financial problems caused a rapid change in its programme from classical music to music hall as the crowds stayed away. It was never a success and has been much altered, including the replacement of its original glass roof with corrugated iron, and is now known as the Plaza. The resort also contained a string of hotels and public houses, many of them along Front Street, the original wide Georgian main street. The architecture of the seven Front Street pubs shows an interesting response to the seaside situation, but is far from seaside architecture as it is usually understood, that is a colourful mixture of bow windows, decorative ironwork and nautical oddments. Front Street, of course, has no direct sea view except at its eastern end, as these only became fashionable at the end of the eighteenth century.

THE PUBS OF FRONT STREET

ROYAL SOVEREIGN-BATH HOTEL

Hidden behind the Arcade on the south side of Front Street is the Royal Sovereign, known before 1967 as the Bath Hotel after the nearby nineteenth century baths at Prior's Haven, below the Priory. It originated as an eighteenth century coaching inn, and was the centre of social life in the early nineteenth century resort. The proprietor in the 1820s was Mrs Hannah Spurrier, who also had a virtual monopoly of Tynemouth's bathing machines and acted as 'master of ceremonies' at the resort. She put on plays at the Hotel in 1821-6, which were patronised by officers of the garrison, and arranged other social functions.

The Arcade was not covered until 1860, when the bay windows were also added to the Prior's Park facade. The initials on the imposts of the arches in the Arcade include the Percy crescent above the letter 'N' for the Duke of Northumberland. The assembly rooms, just across the Arcade, were built by the Tynemouth Assembly Company around 1869, the date being inscribed above the doorway. East of the assembly rooms was a reading room and racquet court, the whole being built in red brick with a tower, battlements and decorative half-timbering. By 1887 the Hotel had a small bar with a Front Street entrance next to the Arcade, a passage leading through to the main Hotel area on the south front comprising a coffee room, a large dining room and the usual guest rooms in the three storey red brick building. The front bar had a tiny snug just behind it

which measured only about 8ft. x 11ft. In 1901 the bar and snug were combined to form a new front bar with a semicircular counter, the Front Street elevation repeating the arched pattern of the Arcade with a large curving central window and slightly recessed doors to either side. It was a colourful addition to Front Street, as the facing was faience in shades of pink and red stretching up to the second storey, which had a full width window in three sections. The architects for the alterations were William Hope and J. C. Maxwell, who also worked together on alterations to the Plaza. Hope had offices in both Newcastle and North Shields, and was responsible for the design of many terraced houses in the expanding towns of Tynemouth and North Shields around the turn of the century. He did occasional pub work, and also higher quality housing, as on the Graham Park estate in Gosforth around 1905. These houses show his liking for extra decorative touches, even in domestic work.

The Hotel and the assembly rooms were split up in 1910, the assembly rooms continuing in use until the late 1960s as banqueting rooms and then briefly being a Vaux pub, the Mercedes. The racquet court and assembly rooms are now disused but intact, although the interiors have been changed; the racquet court was still in use at the turn of the century. The Hotel was taken over by Newcastle Breweries after the Second World War and renovated, a second renovation taking place in May 1967 when the Hotel became the Royal Sovereign, after Lord Collingwood's ship at the Battle of Trafalgar. Collingwood, who was born in Newcastle upon Tyne, is commemorated by the Collingwood Monument (1842-9) overlooking the Tyne just south of the Hotel; the guns of the Royal Sovereign are mounted on its base. Hope and Maxwell's Front Street elevation of the Hotel has sadly disappeared, the main entrance of the pub now being via the Arcade.

SALUTATION INN

The only pub with an elevation on the south side of Front Street is the Salutation Inn, a coaching inn dating back to before 1790 and constructed out of two separate houses. It originally had a coach house and stabling for 24 horses. Its interior was made up of four small sitting rooms and a front bar, an arrangement popular with Tynemouth's businessmen in the first half of the twentieth century as two of these rooms were for men only. The Padded Cell and Hell's Kitchen were used for debates and discussions, the Padded Cell having high-backed leather seats around its walls. Hell's Kitchen was 'The Sally's' original kitchen and retained its range.

Jack Mitchell became landlord after the First World War, taking over from his father who had bought the pub in the early years of the century. Mitchell junior retained the licence until 1964, making no significant alterations to the interior, but it was then sold to J. Nimmo & Sons of Castle Eden, who themselves had just been taken over by Whitbreads. They eventually stripped out the collection of small rooms to leave a single large space, although the exterior is much as it was in Victorian times with its shop-style front and decorative pilasters.

CUMBERLAND ARMS

The Cumberland Arms, a piece of red brick and

23. Cumberland Arms

faience Victorian gothic, is the most westerly of the pubs on the north side of Front Street. Its appearance today results from three periods of building, in 1898, 1934 and the early 1960s (see Plate 23). The major 1898 rebuilding was undertaken by W. B. Reid & Co., the architect being F. R. N. Haswell. The pre-1898 pub consisted of a front bar and a rear smoke room and sitting room, reached by a passage to one side of the bar. It was a long, narrow site, and Haswell chose to omit any internal corridors in order to create more bar space (access to the back of the pub was also possible via an external passage). His plan bore little resemblance to the old lay-out, providing for three separate rooms and a bottle and jug. Its most unusual feature was an octagonal buffet (see Fig. 19). The elevation as seen today is striking, with three ogee arches framing two doors and a central window. Above the decorative cornice is a faience panel in brown, yellow and green which includes the name of the pub. The second floor is dominated by a bay window, and the three storey building is topped with

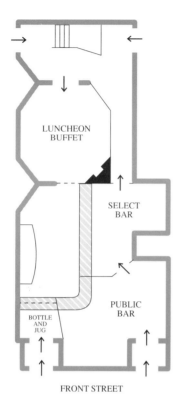

19. Cumberland Arms, 1898 design by
F. R. N. Haswell; (from NTPD)

a gable and three ball finials.

The Front Street facade has undergone no further alterations except the addition of some 1930s glazing, but the interior was remodelled, again by W. B. Reid and the Haswell practice, in 1934. Haswell & Son left the front bar unchanged, which by this time had lost the partition dividing it into select and public bars and was simply the bar. They enlarged the buffet or sitting room to the rear and in so doing

demolished the octagon. New glazing, some of it still visible, was installed, and the first floor club room was replaced by private accommodation.

W. B. Reid were taken over by William Younger, actually Scottish Brewers, in 1956, and the Cumberland Arms became part of the Scottish and Newcastle empire in 1960 when the merger took place. S & N drastically altered the interior in the early 1960s, taking out the remaining internal partitions and introducing a nautical theme of upper and lower decks, thus making use of the difference in level which existed between the front bar and the higher rear buffet. The front bar counter remained where it had been sited in the 1898 rebuilding.

PERCY ARMS

The old Percy Arms had been in the Hutchinson family since at least the mid-1850s, passing from John Hutchinson to William around the turn of the century before it was taken over by Newcastle Breweries in their Swinburne & Co. guise about 1907. The pub was then a plain three storey brick building with a hipped roof, the only indications of its identity as a pub being a single large plate glass window and a few wood carvings of bunches of grapes. Newcastle Breweries were apparently tenants, as the pub was in the hands of Fail & Co. by 1914, but the Breweries had bought the pub by December 1930 when they applied for permission to rebuild.

Their architects were Joseph Oswald & Son who produced an elevation in dark red brick and red sandstone dressings which was repeated on other 1930s Newcastle Breweries pubs, notably the Railway on the Shields Road near Walkergate Station and the Ship Hotel in central Whitley Bay.

24. Percy Arms

The brickwork mimicked a giant order of pilasters and was set on a red marble plinth; a dentil cornice completed the classical look (see Plate 24). It was a very different design from those of 30 years before, the ornate Victorian era having been succeeded in pub design terms by restrained neo-Georgian, or sometimes neo-Tudor. The intention behind this new look was to give the impression that the pub had changed from a seedy gin palace to a wholesome, family orientated lounge or restaurant; an indoor beer garden. The Temperance Movement combined with the licensing justices and the First World War had forced the brewers to aim at a wider market and to begin to supply food as well as drink.

The example of the reformed pub had been set by the wartime Liquor Control Board which had bought the pubs of Carlisle, near the munitions town of Gretna, as a means of controlling workers' drinking. It had closed many pubs and reformed the rest, transforming their appearance by removing the lights and advertising from the outside and the partitions from the inside, and installing extra seating. The Carlisle pubs tended to be anonymous boxes, but pub architects interpreted their post-war brief more widely to include everything from Art Deco to Spanish and more. The new reformed pub was large and often located in the suburbs with ample parking for the car-borne drinker and his family. The brewers liked the neo-Tudor style because of its associations with the old English inn, but architects preferred neo-Georgian, a formal reaction to late Victorian picturesque. The Foxhunters, on Rake Lane just north of Preston, typifies the inter-war neo-Georgian pub.

The interior of the new Percy Arms had four large bars, all served from three small counters grouped together on the Hotspur Street side of the building. Apart from the select room, the bars had new names befitting the new era: the lounge, lounge bar and mixed room. The intended atmosphere was one of restrained relaxation, the rich country house effect being heightened by interior decoration, with wood panelling replacing tiles and Lincrusta paper. Although most of the Percy Arms' interior was altered by an early 1960s S & N renovation, the basic disposition of the rooms has been retained and the wood panelling in the corner lounge remains intact.

THE BAXTER

Just across Hotspur Street from the Percy Arms is the Baxter, the latest addition to the pubs of Front Street. It is owned by Sir John Fitzgerald Ltd., the last surviving Tyneside pub-owning wine and spirit merchants, and like many of their usually inconspicuous pubs could almost be mistaken for a private house. The two storey brick building was still known as Baxter's Cafe in 1968, the subsequent change of use to a pub retaining the name, a dialect version of baker.

THE TURKS HEAD HOTEL

The Turks Head is the most easterly pub on Front Street, and is perhaps best known for being the home of Wandering Willie, the stuffed dog. The pub was owned in 1875 by John Harper Graham, the Newcastle brewer and wine and spirit merchant whose firm was registered in 1900 as J. H. Graham Ltd. Graham owned 7 pubs in the mid-1870s, but sold the Turks Head in 1778 for £6000 to John Hunter, who went bankrupt within two years. The wine and spirit merchants Reid Brothers then took it over, the pub passing to W. B. Reid in 1891 on the incorporation of that company. The Tynemouth innkeeper A. N. Dodds and his son William ran the pub for Reids in the early twentieth century, William becoming manager on the death of his father in 1904; Reids took full control before the First World War.

The Hotel as bought by Reid Brothers had a ground floor bar fitted out with a counter 100ft. long, 60ft. of which was marble covered. Around the marble tables was crimson velvet seating, and on the first floor were smoke and billiard rooms, a bar and a snug. The three storey building had a dining room on its top floor. By 1905, when Reids brought in their usual architect F. R. N. Haswell to make some alterations, the ground floor bar had been split up into a front bar with three sections, a rear sitting room and two bottle and jugs. Haswell provided a sitting room at the front of the pub, placing it to the right of the new central door with the bar to the left, a common arrangement (see Fig. 20). It was still a long bar, stretching the length of the site, but although Haswell retained a separate sitting room at the rear of the pub he removed the snob screens

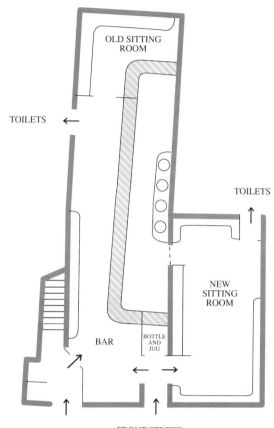

25. *Turks Head Hotel*

20. *Turks Head Hotel, 1905 design by*
F. R. N. Haswell; (from NTPD)

which had been in place on that section of the bar counter. At this time the exterior of the pub was probably painted brick, and there was a first floor ironwork balcony.

The ground floor was unchanged in 1930 when Haswell & Son built a new refreshment room on to

the first floor; the pub was then run by the Elsdon family, who managed it for Reids between the wars. The most noticeable modernisation of the Hotel probably took place in the late 1930s, when the white faience facade was added and the ground floor bars altered. Slabs of white faience now cover all three storeys, the only obvious decoration being cornices at ground and second floor levels. It is a startlingly bright exterior which reflects the clear seaside light; black window frames contrast with the facade, as do the black and white Art Deco doors (see Plate 25). The contemporary glazing in the ground floor windows of the front bar shows that the inter-war alterations restored the nineteenth century plan, with a single front bar and side entrances. The interior of the Hotel has since undergone further changes but the exterior remains crisp and untouched by the salty air.

THE GIBRALTAR ROCK

The Gibraltar Rock overlooks King Edward's Bay and Tynemouth Priory from East Street, the seaward end of Front Street. It was recorded as being in existence in 1827, but today's pub is an amalgamation of the two inns, the Gibraltar Rock and the Priory, which stood on the site (separated by a cottage) until 1927. The Priory was the more northerly of the two inns. Mrs Mavis Carruthers, who owned the pub until 1954, converted the buildings and the pub was used by the Tynemouth Golden Sands Club, a charity, as its headquarters for many years. Fund raising sometimes involved sticking bank notes to the walls and ceiling of one of the pub's rooms. In the mid-1930s the pub had four small bars and a dance hall, which was on the site of the Priory Inn. Hammond's United Breweries, and thus eventually Bass, took over the pub when Mrs Carruthers sold up. They undertook a major renovation in 1964 when the interior was completely modernised, but the exterior remained almost unaltered; it is now covered by a pale yellow render.

Although the Bath Hotel is the pub which traditionally catered for Tynemouth's tourist trade, the only Front Street pub which might look out of place were it not at the seaside is the Turks Head with its shining white facade resisting the elements. It is a product of the 1930s as is the Percy Arms, the main periods of modernisation in Front Street being the turn of the century, the 1930s and the 1960s. Apart from some interior decoration themes there is little that relates these pubs to the seaside, although the Gibraltar Rock does make the most of its view. The policy of the large brewers has generally been to continue with a house style rather than respond to wider architectural concerns, Newcastle Breweries in particular taking this approach. In the inter-war years they developed a design policy for marketing their beer which took in all aspects of sales such as packaging, delivery vehicles and, of course, pubs. The Percy Arms 'series' of pubs was produced by the Oswald practice for the Breweries at this time.

The Front Street pubs may not be seaside architecture but they certainly have the colour and variety which is associated with the sea front. From the elegant wood panelling of the Percy Arms to the white faience of the Turks Head, they display the work of architects seeking to use the image of the pub to bring in customers for the brewers.

CHAPTER FIVE

On the South Bank

Felling

FELLING lies just to the east of Gateshead on the south bank of the River Tyne. Most of the Felling area was farmland until the early nineteenth century although Felling itself was a coal mining village. A deep pit had been sunk there in 1779 to take advantage of the increased demand for coal to be shipped to London, and the industry continued to expand well into the twentieth century. The chemical industry was Felling's other main employer, the production of alkali on Tyneside beginning at the Walker works in 1796 and continuing until the local system was overtaken by technical progress in the 1870s.

Late Victorian Felling stretched from High Felling, the largest part of the village, down the hill to Low Felling on the far side of the Sunderland Road and then to Felling Shore on the river bank. The High Street dropped 80ft. northwards from Victoria Square to the main road and the railway, where a new station had been opened in 1896. In 1894 High Felling had nine public houses, nearly all sited round Victoria Square or on the Sunderland Road, as well as seven beer retailers; most of the pubs

are still functioning today.

Architecturally, Felling's pubs stand out because of the presence of some surprisingly large corner towers and domes. Big pubs are only to be expected in a heavy industrial area where small, early nineteenth century pubs have been rebuilt, but four pubs seem to have competed to present the strongest, most striking images, signifying both wealth and respectability as their facades attempted to remind prospective customers of grand public buildings. The smaller pubs are also of interest, particularly the Bay Horse and the Wheatsheaf in High and Low Felling respectively. The Bay Horse is a 1901 design by Benjamin Simpson, while the Wheatsheaf was rebuilt for Newcastle Breweries in 1907, but the architect is unknown. Intriguingly, given the interesting designs of the Felling pubs, not all the architects have yet been identified, but it is usually possible to make a suggestion on the basis of the style adopted for rebuilding.

Of the nine pubs still standing in the area of Felling High Street, six are worthy of detailed consideration because of their architect or design.

THE BAY HORSE

The Bay Horse, just to the south of Victoria Square on Coldwell Street, was rebuilt soon after April 1901 for John White of the Felling innkeepers White and Bennett. Simpson's design was for a two storey building with a stone facade in a mildly Georgian style, its only decorative features being small canopies over the two front doors. The pub was built as originally planned, but one of the canopies has since disappeared and only a single door is in use. The design is unspectacular, and as such was possibly the result of a request from the client; certainly Simpson had already produced more visually interesting designs, for example the unbuilt 1898 version of the Cumberland Arms in Byker (see Chapter 2) and the Lord Clyde, also in Byker at the east end of the Shields Road. The latter pub, designed in 1896 for Gateshead brewers John Rowell & Sons, has a pair of windows whose basic rectangular shape has been altered by the addition at the top of a semicircular portion. The adjacent deep semicircles give an arcade-like effect (more noticeable before modern reglazing).

Simpson began his own architectural practice in 1889, at first doing most of his work for local brewers rebuilding and altering their pubs. Perhaps as a result of this early experience, Simpson became an eclectic designer, able to produce facades in any style or a mixture of many, and usually more concerned with the facade than the interior, which in any case would normally include many fittings ordered straight from manufacturers' catalogues. He used suppliers from all over England, the domes of the art nouveau Emerson Chambers originating in London. Simpson's work after Emerson Chambers and the

1904 Half Moon went into decline, his preference for decorative facades being overtaken by the trend towards plainer neo-Georgian; he gradually ceased practising during the early 1910s.

PORTLAND ARMS

The Bay Horse may not be the only Simpson pub in Felling, as there is a possibility that the Portland Arms, or the Shakespeare Inn as it was previously known, is also his work. It is sited on Split Crow Road and was one of the three inns which existed in Felling in 1824; it was rebuilt for John White in 1898. The rebuilding resulted in a three storey red brick building with stone dressings and a dramatic green copper dome on its chamfered corner (see Plate 26). The ground floor windows are deep semicircles and a few letters of the original name are still visible under the new paintwork.

The suspicion that it is a Simpson design arises as the client was John White, as with the Bay Horse, and both a dome and deep semicircular windows are part of the design. The windows are very like the original windows of the Lord Clyde, designed by Simpson just two years before the Shakespeare Inn rebuilding (see Plate 27). The dome is not high but is wide in relation to the proportions of the building, and could have acted as a trial for Simpson's later use of complex domes on Emerson Chambers. Domes and deep semicircular windows are not uncommon motifs in turn of the century pub design, but their use in a John White pub may point to Simpson as being the architect.

Across Split Crow Road on the corner of Victoria Square is the Victoria Jubilee, a two storey sandstone building with rusticated quoins. It was

26. Portland Arms

known as the Barley Mow until 1887 when it was bought by John White and renamed in honour of the Queen's jubilee.

BLUE BELL

Victoria Square is dominated by the three storey red brick bulk of the Blue Bell, rebuilt in 1903-5 by Newcastle Breweries (see Plate 28). It is a large corner pub with deep semicircular windows, stone window dressings and two stone door canopies; its gabled roof is topped by tall chimney-stacks and a black wooden cupola. A terracotta plaque over a High Street corner window gives 1905 as the date of

rebuilding, when the pub was run as a Swinburne house. It is possible that the Oswald practice could be responsible for the design, as they frequently worked for Newcastle Breweries around the turn of the century, but this seems stylistically improbable. Although the practice produced pub designs in a wide variety of styles, the facades were normally much more decorative than the plain red brick of the Blue Bell. The windows are reminiscent of those of the Portland Arms, but Simpson does not seem to have worked for the Breweries; the architect is currently unknown.

The old Blue Bell was the home for many years of the Felling Hoppings, which took place annually

27. *Lord Clyde*

28. *Blue Bell*

on Whit Monday. The fair was held in the yard of the pub and out on the square, where the greasy pole was erected (see Plate 29). By about 1904 the rides included gondolas and roundabouts, but in 1908 the fair moved from the newly rebuilt pub to a larger site nearby at the foot of Booth Street.

About half way down the High Street between the Blue Bell and Low Felling stands the Half Way House, a Sir John Fitzgerald pub. It is a two storey, five bay stone building with a dark pink stucco facade and pairs of fluted wooden ionic pilasters decorating the doorcases. It is the oldest surviving pub in the High Street and was improved in 1900 after John Fitzgerald bought it, having run it since at least 1894.

BEESWING

The Beeswing dominates the lower end of the High Street, its green domed tower looking out over the junction with the Sunderland Road. The tower, above a chamfered corner, has an open black wooden drum below its dome which is capped with a finial. The pub was rebuilt in 1899 for Robert Deuchar & Co. by Benjamin Simpson, who produced a picturesque three storey red brick composition which included dormer, oriel and deep semicircular windows (see Plate 30). These latter are very similar to the ground floor windows of both the Blue Bell, which the Beeswing predates by about four years, and the Shakespeare Inn, the possible Simpson design of 1898. The rebuilding applications for the Shakespeare Inn and the Beeswing were presented within four months of each other in 1898, and given the similarities between the designs, it seems highly likely that Simpson was responsible for

29. Hoppings in the old Blue Bell yard, about 1900 (GLAD)

both. The Beeswing was fitted out by a selection of Newcastle firms, mainly working from the prestigious furniture making area around Pilgrim Street and Northumberland Street. Burroughes & Watts supplied the billiard table, and the cabinet making was carried out by Lorentz Gullaschen, whose main works were at Sandyford Road, close to the Deuchar brewery. Little of the Victorian interior remains today.

The Beeswing was given its name by the original owner Joseph Drummond, who sold up in the late 1850s. Beeswing was a horse owned by Mr Orde of Nunnykirk in Northumberland which won 51 races, including the Ascot Gold Cup in 1842, the Doncaster Cup (four times) and the Newcastle Cup (six times). A very tough mare, she was idolised by northern racegoers; many songs were written and inns named in her honour. After her racing career she became one of the most influential of all stud mares.

Drummond sold the Beeswing to John Stephenson, and it was being run by Farquhar

30. Beeswing

31. Royal Turf

Deuchar & Co. in 1894. Farquhar was a son of Robert who had started an innkeeping business around 1887. He eventually joined his father's firm on 18 January 1898, his pubs then becoming Robert Deuchar houses. During the 1920s the licensee of the Beeswing was Tommy Burns, the French Canadian who was world heavyweight boxing champion in 1906-8. He set up a boxing ring in one of the upstairs rooms of the pub during his tenancy.

ROYAL TURF

Just to the east of the Beeswing along the

Sunderland Road is the Royal Turf, another Simpson pub with the combination of a tower and deep semicircular windows (see Plate 31). The tower in this case is a large corner oriel window, overlooked by the rose window of St Patrick's Roman Catholic church on the High Street above. The pub was originally known as the Turf Hotel, and was run in 1892 by John B. Makepeace, a mineral water manufacturer of Felling. Soon after that date it came into the hands of Farquhar Deuchar, and thence passed to Robert Deuchar in 1898, by which time it was known as the Royal Turf. As with the Beeswing, plans for rebuilding were drawn up only a few months after the pub changed hands, and the pub was closed for building work by mid-1899. The rebuilding was carried out by Newcastle builder John Hope, and many of the firms which worked on fitting out the Beeswing were also used at the Royal Turf. The pub was open again by early 1900. Its facade is not as flamboyant as those of the Shakespeare Inn or the Beeswing and is dominated by the tower window; on the first floor the heavy wooden ribbed ceiling of the tower room still remains intact. Unfortunately the tower window was boarded over internally in 1988, giving the previously striking corner a rather blank appearance. Simpson's use of towers, domes and fenestration in the Beeswing, the Royal Turf and (possibly) the Shakespeare Inn shows how simple elements can be combined to produce an impressive variety of arresting elevations, particularly suitable for corner pubs. The designs were all completed in 1898 but each elevation is quite different, emphasising Simpson's interest in exciting facades. The Royal Turf eventually became a Bass pub, after a period in S & N ownership.

WHEATSHEAF

North of the grand towers of High Felling is an equally interesting but much smaller scale pub, the Wheatsheaf in Low Felling. It stands on the east side of Carlisle Street, the continuation of the High Street across the main road, and was rebuilt by Newcastle Breweries to plans drawn up in 1906. The old Wheatsheaf was owned by John Barras & Co. and became a Newcastle Breweries property when the company was formed in 1890. It was a two storey end-terrace building faced in coursed stone, the first floor being supported by a column where the ground floor corner was chamfered (see Plate 32). It was an ordinary street corner pub, but on rebuilding was turned by an unknown architect into a fine example of Edwardian pub design.

The pub today stands isolated, but retains its column and chamfered corner. The facade is now largely faience and red brick, the yellow and green faience covering the ground floor and the column. On the first floor is a small triangular oriel window, and the gable is decorated with a wheat sheaf and the rebuilding date 1907 (see Plate 33). The style is a combination of Arts and Crafts and neo-Georgian, the dentil cornice and gable detailing being more formal than the flowing, coloured ground floor. Many Arts and Crafts architects used formal elements in their late Victorian house designs, and neo-Georgian was popular for Edwardian domestic work; the Wheatsheaf design reflects this change of emphasis from informal to formal, although at a later stage than in domestic design. The Wheatsheaf facade has much in common with that of Crane House at New Quay, North Shields, designed by Joseph Oswald & Son in 1904 for Newcastle Breweries (see Chapter 3). The large gable, tall chimney-stack, dentil cornice, oriel window, chamfered corner and ground floor faience facing are all common to both, although the Wheatsheaf is a rather more formal composition. It seems probable that the Oswald practice was responsible for the Wheatsheaf design, as it was drawn up for Newcastle Breweries and has so many

32. Left: Wheatsheaf, Felling, before rebuilding (GLAD)
33. Right: Wheatsheaf

similarities with their Crane House design.

The interior of the pub is still almost as originally designed, although the side porch, which divided the front and rear bars, was demolished in spring 1988. The bar counter and back bar fitting are unchanged, as is the relief wallpaper. Embossed wheat sheaves decorate the glass of the rear windows. By 1914, when the total value of Newcastle Breweries' properties was estimated to be £1,041,415, the Wheatsheaf was valued at £2000. The Breweries retained the pub until 1985; it was then sold and now retails the products of Newcastle's Big Lamp brewery, set up in 1982.

Thanks to Benjamin Simpson, the Oswald practice and the pub owners, even a small town like Felling can boast of a number of large and unusual pubs. Pubs have often been ignored as being of little architectural interest or distinction, but even this small sample exhibits trends apparent in domestic and commercial architecture of the late Victorian and Edwardian era, and are thus part of the mainstream of English design. Perhaps they are most important as the built expression of the fortunes of the drink trade over the last century, including towering expansion and sedate contraction.

CHAPTER SIX

Out in the Country

Weardale

UNLIKE the city pub, the country pub usually has few architectural pretensions and is typically a larger version of the vernacular housing to be found locally. In Weardale, where Carboniferous limestone and Coal Measures sandstone are the dominant building materials, variations on the theme of a three bay, two to three storey stone built pub are common. The windows may be accentuated by means of architraves painted in a colour contrasting with the stuccoed walls, and the roofs are often sandstone flagged.

Weardale itself was and is an industrial valley, at its productive peak towards the end of the nineteenth century when lead and iron ore were mined and limestone quarried. The towns of the valley were bases for the mining and quarrying companies, Stanhope and Wolsingham also being important market towns. The number of pubs in the dale has changed little since the end of the nineteenth century except in the case of Wolsingham, where following the 1904 Licensing Act the licensing justices took a hard line and reduced the number of pubs by half in the period leading up to the Second World War.

WOLSINGHAM

Wolsingham was the market town for Lower Weardale and lies at its eastern end. The railway reached Wolsingham when the Wear Valley Railway opened its line from Bishop Auckland to Frosterley on 3 August 1847. By 1891 the population was about 2600 and three years later there were twelve pubs, seven of them clustered round the Market Place, as well as a wine and spirit merchant, Thomas Wiseman. Today there are only five, the most architecturally interesting being the Black Bull in the Market Place, a grade II listed building dating from the mid-eighteenth century. Its white painted and incised stucco facade hides most of its sandstone construction, although the stone is visible in a gable end. The most unusual pub of the five is the Grey Bull, which was rebuilt in 1927 using the then fashionable neo-Georgian style with touches of Arts and Crafts decorative brickwork (see Plate 34). The hipped roof and white pebbledashed facade emphasise its suburban appearance, contrasting with

34. Grey Bull

the vernacular of the Wear Valley Inn at the east end of the town.

The King's Head, with its row of three ground floor bay windows, has expanded since the turn of the century when it had a single bay windowed bar, a snug and a sitting room. In 1904 it belonged to North Eastern Breweries, who owned five pubs in Wolsingham just before the First World War. North Eastern Breweries was originally the Spennymoor firm of Bramwell & Co, founded in 1800; on its incorporation in 1896 it took in a mass of small breweries from Sunderland, Middlesbrough, Stockton on Tees and Burton. It was acquired by C. Vaux & Sons Ltd. of Sunderland in 1927, the company being known as Associated Breweries, but continued to trade under its own name until 1950. Associated Breweries was renamed Vaux and Associated Breweries in 1940.

North Eastern Breweries, then Vaux, became the dominant pub owners in Wolsingham during the early twentieth century when many pubs were being closed by the licensing justices in order to further temperance reform. The 1904 Licensing Act provided for the payment of compensation to owners, lessees and licensees of pubs closed when their licences were terminated as they fell due for renewal, the compensation being obtained from a levy on all pubs in the county. In 1907 the justices closed the Royal Oak, a Market Place beerhouse leased by Hartlepool brewers J. W. Cameron & Co. It was almost a year before the compensation payment was settled, Camerons receiving £298.10.0 and the licensee £35. In 1909 two more pubs were shut, the Farmers Rest, a beerhouse, and the Blue Bell Inn, a Market Place pub leased by James Deuchar; the closure was opposed but to no avail, Deuchar only obtaining £80 compensation although the owner was granted £1090.

The brewers were coming under increasing financial pressure through taxation, the compensation levy, loss of sales to clubs and the closure of public houses. In April 1911 a deputation from the Northumberland and Durham Brewers' Association and the National Trade Defence Association attended the Durham County Licensing Committee to put forward their views on compensation. The deputation included Major Ernest Vaux and representatives of North Eastern Breweries, James Calder & Co. of Alloa and J. Nimmo & Sons, but the closures continued after a wartime respite. The Golden Lion, a coaching inn close to the Black Bull and now a doctor's surgery, was shut in 1923. The compensation due to the landlord was instead paid to the Haughton Road Brewery Co. of Darlington, later part of John Smith's Tadcaster Brewery Co. Ltd., to whom the landlord was in debt. The North Eastern Breweries' Wheatsheaf was closed in 1928, followed in 1930 by the seventeenth century Queen's Head (now three houses in the Market Place) and the Pack Horse, owned by the West Auckland Brewery Co. Ltd. and Bentley's Yorkshire Breweries of Woodlesford, West Yorkshire, respectively. By the 1930s only two pubs remained in the Market Place. Although this represented a success for the licensing justices, it had the probably unanticipated effect of reducing the choice of beer available in Wolsingham, as brewers with a single pub in the town preferred the busy Market Place site. Apart from North Eastern Breweries only Camerons, with the Royal Oak and the Black Lion (still in existence), owned or leased more than one pub in the town before the closures.

When altering or rebuilding their pubs, North Eastern Breweries normally used an architect from the town in which the pub was situated, although Thomas H. Murray of Consett did a great deal of work for the company, some of it non-local, between the turn of the century and the Second World War. He drew up plans for minor alterations to the King's Head at Wolsingham in 1904. After 1940, W. & T. R. Milburn of Sunderland were used by the firm, who by then were part of Vaux. The Milburn practice had produced the Porthole on North Shield's New Quay, and Stanley Milburn, later a partner in his own right, had overall responsibility for the architecture of the North-East Coast Exhibition held at Newcastle in 1929. Its style was a theatrical neo-classical, reminiscent of a film set and in the tradition of the theatres designed by the practice at the turn of the century.

FROSTERLEY

Frosterley had four pubs in 1894, but is now reduced to one, the grade II listed Frosterley Inn, a Vaux house dating from the mid-eighteenth century (see Plate 35). The three bay, three storey building is faced in pale yellow painted stucco with contrasting architraves, quoins and doorcase; it has a Welsh slate roof. The four nineteenth century pubs catered for the quarry workers who made up most of the population of the town. Two new limestone quarries, at Stanhope and Parson Byers, midway between Frosterley and Stanhope, had been opened soon after the railway was extended from Frosterley to Stanhope. The line opened on 22 October 1862 and was worked by the Stockton & Darlington Railway, the local line's parent company. Although mineral production continued in Upper Weardale during the latter part of the nineteenth century, it was

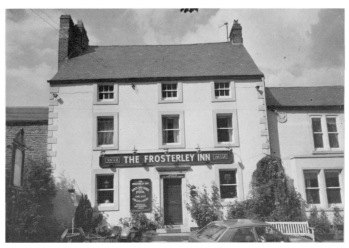

35. Frosterley Inn

21 October 1895 before the railway covered the remaining $9^1/_4$ miles to Wearhead, and by this time the industry in the whole of Weardale had gone into a decline. In spite of this all four Frosterley pubs - the Hare and Hounds, the Black Bull, the Railway Tavern and the Foresters' Arms - were still functioning in 1925.

STANHOPE

Late nineteenth century Stanhope was the market town for Upper Weardale, boasting five pubs and a hotel as well as the mineral water makers and beer bottlers Joseph and Thomas Robinson. The Robinsons produced such delights as zolaade, champagne cider, horehound (a cough remedy) and Lithia water (prescribed for gout) in addition to the usual soft drinks. The Phoenix (now inexplicably the Bonny Moor Hen) was a family and commercial

hotel in the nineteenth century, and stands on the north side of the Market Place, opposite the Pack Horse Inn. These two pubs both date from the late eighteenth century and are grade II listed buildings constructed of sandstone, the Phoenix in ashlar and the Pack Horse in coursed rubble. Later additions to the Pack Horse include a glazed ground floor verandah facing the Market Place. Both Red and White Lions have disappeared since the turn of the century but the Grey Bull and the Queen's Head remain, the Grey Bull being of rather urban appearance with its large ground floor windows.

UPPER WEARDALE

The Cross Keys at Eastgate was originally two houses, of early to mid-eighteenth century date, and is listed grade II. It is a two and a half storey sandstone building with a flagged roof, and still has two 'Yorkshire' horizontally sliding sash windows in its top storey. These were inferior to the vertical sash, but were used particularly for square windows before the vertical variety became commonplace. Little original glazing remains in many Weardale pubs; the introduction of two dimensional mock Georgian glazing has led to a marked change for the worse in their appearance.

The Hare and Hounds at Westgate is the one survivor there from the nineteenth century, when the Miners' Arms and the Half Moon also served the population of 820. The landlords of the Miners' Arms and the Hare and Hounds took on other jobs to make a living, as stone mason and joiner respectively; this practice was not uncommon in Weardale, mirroring the combination of lead mining and farming which was pursued by many of the local smallholders.

Three of the four St John's Chapel pubs are vernacular buildings, two or three storey stone buildings with little decoration except, in the case of the King's Arms, a doorcase with curious four-leafed clover designs in the upper corners of the architrave. The fourth, the early eighteenth century Golden Lion, is a two storey mixture of sandstone and limestone with a stone flagged roof, and is listed grade II. Its most interesting feature is a somewhat vernacular version of a Venetian window on its front facade, that is a window with three openings, the central one arched. The heavy stone architrave merely emphasises the point that this motif is usually seen on rather more elegant Palladian houses.

Wearhead, the end of the railway line, no longer has a pub although the Queen's Head was in existence in 1894, its landlord Isaac Thompson also being a joiner. Although little more than a village,

nineteenth century Wearhead had two chapels, the Primitive Methodist (1823) and the Wesleyan (1871), which between them could seat 850 people. Methodism had become the strongest religion in the dales largely because of the difficulty in attending the old parish churches, far away from the new mining villages. Cowshill, almost at the head of Weardale, still has one pub the Cowshill Hotel, a two and a half storey vernacular building in white rendered stone. The village had a lead mine at the turn of the century, owned by the Weardale Lead Company which took over the Beaumont Company's mines in Weardale after mining became uneconomic in the 1890s. Cowshill's pub was then known as the Free Masons' Arms.

The pubs of Weardale are almost all plain vernacular buildings, but as with the more fashionable urban pubs, their history reflects directly the vagaries of the local economy and national trends concerning temperance and brewery mergers. Pubs in the smaller dales towns and villages are often still free houses, but generally obtain their beer from one of the larger brewers. Choice, both in terms of beer and pubs, has decreased since the turn of the century but the continuing and possibly now increasing demand for pubs and hotels ensures that the buildings themselves are used for their original, or at least secondary, purpose. The vernacular country pub may not have the architectural excitement of the town pub, but it often has a longer history.

CHAPTER SEVEN

Along the North Tyne

THE typical pub of the picturesque North Tyne valley is a two, sometimes three, storey sandstone building in roughly coursed stone with a slate roof. Unlike the Weardale pubs there are no decorative architraves, but the stone is sometimes rendered and painted; in Bellingham there has even been a recent outbreak of black and white half timbering! In general, the pubs in existence today are those which were there in the late nineteenth century, albeit with the occasional change of name; there was no industrial decline in the North Tyne valley to precipitate pub closures as in Weardale.

Bellingham's ironstone works and the coal from Plashetts, just to the north of what is now the Kielder Reservoir, were the main reasons for the construction of the railway up the valley in 1855-6 by the North British Railway. The railway carried passenger traffic as well as goods, and brought extra trade to local inns; the George at Chollerford, an early Georgian coaching inn, was just across the bridge from the new Humshaugh station. The George is now much enlarged, but where the ivy has

not completely covered its exterior a Venetian window may be seen overlooking the North Tyne. The inn was once part of the great Chesters Estate owned by the Clayton family of Chesters, the house just to the west of Chollerford built by John Clayton in 1771 and extravagantly remodelled for Nathaniel Clayton by Richard Norman Shaw in 1891-4. Much of the estate, including the George, was sold off in 1929 when the annual rental on the inn was only £156. The inn had stabling for four horses and garages for three cars; a point of equilibrium before the car took over.

The Hadrian at Wall, across the line of Hadrian's Wall to the south of Chollerford, was also part of the Chesters Estate sold in 1929, when it was known as the Smith's Arms. It was a small pub, the rent being only £19 per annum, and had been bought by the Clayton family from Mrs Sarah Wilkinson of Hexham in 1831, when it was called the Blacksmith's Arms. There were two pubs at Wall in 1894, the Smith's Arms (whose landlord was Smith Urwin, a blacksmith) and the nearby North Tyne Hotel, which between them catered for a population of just over 400. The North Tyne Hotel became a temperance hotel in the late 1920s or 1930s, leaving the Hadrian, renamed and expanded following the sale, as the sole pub in the village.

The Crown at Humshaugh is a two storey three bay stone built pub, its single ground floor bay window being a later addition; its facade is of coursed stone with quoins. It was a coaching inn and is a good example of a vernacular North Tyne valley pub, but the Barrasford Arms, up the valley in Barrasford is completely atypical, a Victorian villa of a pub. Wark's two pubs, the Grey Bull and the Black Bull, lie side by side opposite The Green, an area of common land which cannot be enclosed. The Black Bull is the older and lower of the pair of two storied buildings, and has stone mullioned ground floor windows and a minimal hood-mould above the door. The Grey Bull lacks any decorative touches but is finished with a pale yellow wash.

Bellingham is the largest town in the valley and had four pubs in the late nineteenth century, the Rose and Crown, the Fox and Hounds, the Black Bull and the Railway Hotel. They all remain today, however the Railway Hotel has become the Cheviot and the Fox and Hounds is now disused, although still recognisable. Its most interesting feature is a small plaque above a doorway which reads 'RRL 1731'; the presence of internal shutters suggest that it is indeed a Georgian building, but the date on the plaque might refer not to the construction date but to some important family event. In seventeenth and eighteenth century Yorkshire Dales houses it was usual to carve the building date and family's initials on the lintel of a doorway, but this practice is uncommon in Northumberland where the building stone is easily weathered sandstone rather than the millstone grit of Yorkshire.

Opposite the Fox and Hounds, which was still in use as a pub in the late 1970s, is the Black Bull in its startling disguise of whitewash and black half-timbering. Its landlord in 1894 was one Pierre Varvaet, but by 1938 it had become a Robert Deuchar pub, a narrow three storey building with a bar and two sitting rooms entered from a roughly central porch on Front Street. Deuchar submitted plans to alter the pub in late 1938, using Sidney Lawson of Newcastle to draw up the design. Lawson had been one of Benjamin Simpson's partners, and had taken over the practice about 1913. Lawson suggested a slightly more imposing exterior, with an added gable above the porch, new dormer windows and a separate entrance for one of the sitting rooms, the outside walls to be a light brown cement render. Internally, the service area remained much as it had been, but the bar and sitting rooms were rearranged to provide more comfortable sitting areas, every room having a window on the Front Street facade rather than overlooking the churchyard. Apart from greater comfort there was little reason for change, as the Black Bull was already very much the brewers' idea of a reformed pub, the traditional English inn.

The Rose and Crown stands in the square to the east of the Black Bull, a two storey free house with more decorative half timbering. It underwent slight alteration by a Newcastle architect in 1937, when it had a bar and sitting room facing the square and a small snug to the rear; the basic structure of the building has remained unchanged. Bellingham's fourth pub, the Railway Hotel, is a three bay, three storey stone building recently renamed the Cheviot. As the Railway Hotel it had a front bar and smoke room with a rear snug, all on a larger scale than the other pubs. In 1947 the architects Dixon and Son from Newcastle drew up plans to enlarge the ground floor drinking area by moving the kitchen upstairs, and an open plan lounge cum smoke room was created while leaving the bar and snug almost as they were. As with the Black Bull the redesign emphasised comfort, two new fires being installed in the lounge, one of which replaced the kitchen range.

Upstream from Bellingham the North Tyne valley pubs are small, two storey, stone buildings carrying the names of assorted game birds: the Moorcock at The Eals, the Pheasant at Stannersburn and at Falstone the Blackcock, a Vaux pub previously known as the Black Cock Inn. It stands just to the south of the course of the old North British Railway line. Most of the pubs of the valley are straightforward vernacular architecture, little affected by modern trends in pub design. Even when city architects worked on them in the twentieth century change was not dramatic; almost all the nineteenth century North Tyne valley pubs have survived as working pubs and still look much the same, apart from a little extra ivy or half timbering, as they did at the turn of the century. Rural Northumbrian pubs generally have been altered less than their city equivalents, having escaped the competitive pressures of the brewing industry as more money was to be made from the city pubs.

CHAPTER EIGHT

Vaux and Sunderland

A Vaux brewery has existed in Sunderland since about 1805, when Cuthbert Vaux set up in partnership with a Mr W. Story at their small brewery in Moor Street near the old town centre in the east of the town. This partnership lasted until 1837 when the company C. Vaux & Sons was established at a brewery on the corner of Matlock and Cumberland Streets, just west of the present Wearmouth Bridge. As the business expanded the firm moved first to Union Street and then in 1875 to Castle Street after the North Eastern Railway Company acquired the latter site for the construction of its Central Station. Vaux have remained at Castle Street ever since, the first brew at the new brewery being produced in June 1875. Cuthbert Vaux died in 1878, but the business was already being run by his sons John Story Vaux and Colonel Edwin Vaux. J. S. Vaux died in 1881, his two sons Major Cuthbert Vaux and Colonel Ernest Vaux later becoming partners in the firm, which became a limited company in 1896.

Although Vaux have outlasted Sunderland's other brewers, evolved into a major regional brewing group and remained independent of the giant brewing conglomerates, they do not have a strong holding of owned or tied houses in their home town. This situation has not changed since the company was incorporated, their great strength in pub terms always lying in the old Durham mining areas and further south in Middlesbrough. In 1892 William St John and Annison, one of six or more Sunderland firms which combined the trades of brewer and wine and spirit merchant, were the town's most important owners of on-licence premises in numerical terms with 31 houses. Newcastle Breweries had 28 and only then came Vaux (also a brewer cum wine and spirit merchant) and James Deuchar with 22 each, out of the 417 houses in the borough. Competition between breweries was fierce in the early 1890s, with at least ten breweries having offices or brewing in Sunderland. Brewers owned around half the local pubs, with the 13 brewers who owned two or more pubs accounting for 191 of the total, while other breweries owned single houses. William Jackson, the Sunderland wine and spirit merchants, owned a further 15 houses. Tenants of pubs which were not owned directly by breweries might be tied to a single brewery or free to choose the beer they sold, and here Vaux began with an advantage as they brewed with good quality water and thus produced beer competitive with the Burton ales introduced into the region in the latter part of the nineteenth century. It appears that towards the end of the century Vaux chose to sell their beers by promoting their quality through the free trade, rather than ensuring a market by buying up public houses.

Other brewers were keener to establish themselves in the Sunderland tied house market, James Deuchar for example buying Sir Hedworth Williamson's 22 houses around 1891. Williamson was the principal landowner on the north bank of the Wear, the family having dominated the area from the late seventeenth century; Roker Park was given to the town by the Williamsons in 1880. W. B. Reid of Newcastle also bought into the Sunderland trade around 1891, taking over the eight houses owned by James Chrisp, a local wine and spirit merchant. One of these pubs, the Ship Isis in Silksworth Row, had been rebuilt by Chrisp in 1885 and it is possible that the pub building boom began rather earlier in Sunderland than on Tyneside, where its first peak came in 1890. Certainly Sunderland's industry and population grew dramatically during the mid and late nineteenth century and into the early years of the twentieth, the population almost tripling between 1841 and 1901 when it was about 146,000. Both shipbuilding and coal were expanding industries in the early 1900s, although by the turn of the century the Wearside bottle making industry was in decline, having been overtaken by mechanisation and the rise of overseas competition. The Ayres Quay Bottle Company works, which closed in 1923,

was one of the world's largest during the nineteenth century; W. B. Reid used their bottles while Fenwicks, the Sunderland brewers, owned the Bishopwearmouth Panns bottle works (south east of Wearmouth Bridge) between about 1827 and 1881. The collection of imposing Edwardian pubs which remains in Sunderland today is a reminder of the prosperity and confidence of the town in the early years of the century.

The Ship Isis is a fine example of late Victorian solidity, its stone facade resembling an office or club rather than a pub (see Plate 36). The style is renaissance with a touch of romanesque in the heavy, round-headed second storey windows, and the parapet is pierced with circular holes. The Ship Isis typifies W. B. Reid's Sunderland pubs which were mainly large establishments, and indeed were advertised as hotels, with the emphasis on the variety of rooms available for functions ranging from banquets to billiards; the Reid pubs were all managed by the publican George Bell from the turn of the century until at least the Second World War. Only a quarter mile from the Ship Isis stands the Bee Hive (now Oddies) in Hylton Road, also a product of 1880s rebuilding although on a less grand scale. The entire ground floor exterior has been modernised but the remaining decorative elements on the upper storey indicate that even simple corner pubs were profitable in late Victorian Sunderland. The sandstone dressings include swagged ionic pilasters and, on the gable, a cartouche containing the rebuilding date of 1881 and a perfectly carved beehive which has weathered surprisingly little (see Plate 37). The Bee Hive came under the control of William Jackson (Sunderland) Ltd. in the 1920s, the company formed from the original wine and spirit

36. Ship Isis

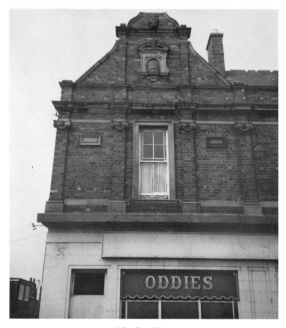

37. Bee Hive

merchants, and then passed to London and Burton brewers Truman, Hanbury, Buxton & Co. Ltd. in the 1930s. The London brewery took over six of the Jackson pubs to give them a foothold in Sunderland, but Jacksons kept the Bridge Hotel in High Street West, an early nineteenth century pub where masonic meetings were held in the 1860s (see Plate 38). Its ground floor facade is partly covered with Victorian ceramic panels and tiling, the best of the tiles having a moulded grapevine design in red,

yellow and green on a blue background. In 1967 Jacksons, who by then owned 12 pubs, were taken over by Tetley Walker Ltd.

The first two decades of the twentieth century saw little growth in the Vaux empire of pubs and breweries. While more brewers moved into the Sunderland market and opened offices in the town, Vaux refrained from takeovers and continued to build its reputation as a stout brewer. By 1906 several local breweries had either gone out of business or been taken over by firms based outside Sunderland. Bramwell & Co. had become part of the Spennymoor-based North Eastern Breweries on its incorporation in 1896, T. E. Chapman had been

The Edwardian competition for drinkers led to the erection of several large and sumptuous pubs in Sunderland in the first decade of the century. Vaux did not participate in this game of architectural showmanship, their pubs being more vernacular buildings than built advertisements. A prime example of the grand Edwardian pub is the Mountain Daisy in Hylton Road, rebuilt for W. B. Reid by Sunderland architects William and T. R. Milburn in 1900-1902. Even before rebuilding the pub had been large, with four sitting rooms, a snug, a bottle and jug and a front bar, but the new pub was almost the size of a small country house, its bulk dominating the road. It is a three storey red brick building with stone dressings and a black marble facing on the ground floor. It has a square corner tower, a series of giant shaped gables, an oriel window and tall chimney-stacks (see Plate 39). The slightly Queen Anne revival style of the pub is emphasised by a metal plaque on the west facade bearing a delicate impression of a mountain daisy;

38. *Bridge Hotel*

taken over by the Hartlepool firm J. W. Cameron in 1897, and R. Fenwick & Co. had been taken over by Alloa brewer George Younger in 1898, although it was still trading as Fenwicks in 1906. George Mackay & Co. of Edinburgh and the Tadcaster Tower Brewery Co. also had offices in Sunderland by 1906, joining Newcastle Breweries and James Deuchar, the only non-local firms with offices in the town in 1892; by the early years of the century, any profits to be made from Sunderland's beer drinkers were generally travelling outside Sunderland.

39. *Mountain Daisy*

the Queen Anne style was noted for its use of red brick, tall, ribbed chimneys, shaped gables and the sunflower as a decorative motif. A plaque on the east facade bears the date of building, 1901; building control records show that roofing was in progress on 21 January 1902. The rebuilt pub retained a similar plan to its predecessor, with a long front bar, in this case divided into three separate sections, two rear sitting rooms, a news room and two family departments (see Fig. 21). It provided ample

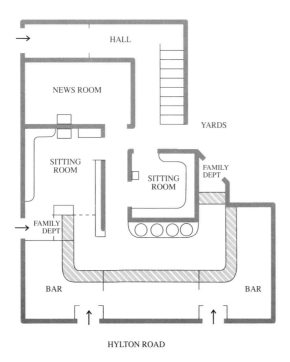

21. Mountain Daisy, 1900 design by
W. and T. R. Milburn;
(from TWA 269/3478-3492 plan 267)

drinking space and sitting areas, all of which were originally served from a single long bar counter. Although most of the pub has now been altered, the sitting room on the west facade remains as it was when converted into a buffet. Its bar is a quarter circle faced with green and yellow glazed faience in an animal head pattern, and the walls are covered with tile pictures of local scenes. This astonishing work, produced by the firm Craven Dunnill of Jackfield in the Ironbridge Gorge, is described in more detail in Chapter 10. The room also retains its original wooden fittings and glass, and so gives a complete picture of a luxurious northern drinking palace in the Edwardian era.

Simultaneously with Reid's erection of the Mountain Daisy, Robert Deuchar engaged B. F. Simpson to draw up plans for rebuilding the Dun Cow on High Street West opposite St Michael's Church. The old pub, a plain 3½ storey building, was pulled down in January 1901 and the new building erected in 1901-2 by Sunderland builder Thomas Pearson Shaftoe, who was paid £2000 for the first year's building work. Simpson's design, built as planned, was for four stories of Edwardian baroque with the inevitable tower marking the corner of the site (see Plate 40). The pub was built of ashlar on a granite plinth and rose exuberantly towards florid Dutch gables carrying scrolls and finials, and variously decorated with 'RD' for the owner or the date 1901. The copper domed tower held a clock and the roof was of Lakeland slate; three doorways had marble nook shafts. The interior consisted of a large front bar and a tiny rear sitting room, delightfully separated by a curving screen. Fortunately the majority of the bar fittings and screens have remained unchanged, and testify to the

40. Dun Cow

high quality of the joiner's skill and the architect's specification, and the size of the owner's purse. The back bar fitting is particularly splendid, a traceried Indo-Gothic web billowing out to form platforms on which bottles can be displayed; it has a distinctly theatrical appearance, although it predates the Milburns' Empire next door by five years.

The Milburns also produced the design for the Bells, a four storey towered giant on the approach to Wearmouth Bridge at the corner of Bridge Street and West Wear Street. It was rebuilt for James Henderson & Sons, local wine and spirit merchants,

in 1902-3. The previous pub on the site had a single long bar divided into four sections, a sitting room and a very tiny snug. The new pub added a ground floor buffet to the bar and sitting room accommodation, and on the first floor was a double height billiard room with two tables. The most outstanding feature of the pub was its baroque corner tower (see Plate 41). The Bells came into the hands of William Younger & Co. of Edinburgh about 1910, just as they were starting a sales drive in northern England. Youngers held seven Sunderland pubs in 1910, and had the largest tied house trade of any Scottish brewer before the First World War.

The Londonderry Hotel, the largest of the Edwardian giants, dominates a triangular site a few yards to the east of the Dun Cow in High Street West. It was planned in 1901 by Sunderland architect Hugh Hedley for Newcastle brewers Duncan & Daglish. It is a powerful landmark mainly because of its size rather than the qualities of the design, which was required to be in keeping with the proposed municipal buildings on nearby sites; the north west facade of the pub is nine bays in length and the east eight bays. It is built of ashlar and the style is quietly baroque, with lead ogee domes crowning each point of the triangle (see Plate 42).

Even the smaller Edwardian pub could be architecturally distinguished, as B. F. Simpson showed in his rebuilding of the Half Moon in High Street East, carried out in 1903-4. The work was commissioned by Fenwicks (by then George Younger) and involved improving and re-fronting the original pub, which was itself an adaptation of a three story pre-Georgian house. The interior design changed only slightly, retaining a front bar and rear sitting room, a common plan in Sunderland and one

41. The Bells, Bridge Street, Sunderland (SMAG)

42. Londonderry

also used by Simpson at the Grey Horse, rebuilt for Fenwicks in High Street East at the same time. The exterior, however, allowed Simpson to demonstrate what could be achieved with a narrow site. The ground floor, although basically a not unusual arrangement of pilasters between rectangular windows, was faced with blue and yellow faience, the ionic pilasters being crowned with crescent moons. The cornice bearing the pub's name was surmounted by a giant open-topped pediment, into which fitted a two storey oriel window topped with an ogee dome and finial. It was a charming design, but it has not survived; the building ceased to be a pub before the Second World War and was eventually demolished, the faience facade being exported to the United States in the early 1970s. All that remains is the mark of its tall chimney on the gable end of the building to the west, 201 High Street East, part of which was once the Eagle Tavern. A record of the final days of the Half Moon does exist in the form of a 1963 drawing by L. S. Lowry which shows, with some artistic licence, the boarded-up pub (see Plate 43). Lowry was a frequent visitor to the north east, taking his annual holiday at the Seaburn Hotel, Whitburn (built by the Milburns in 1937) from 1964 until his death in 1976.

The Milburns also produced a spectacular small pub in the Edwardian period, the Hat and Feather in Low Row, once known as the Green Room and now simply as Greens. The pub was designed for local wine and spirit merchants Charles Green & Co. in June 1903 by the brothers William (1858-1935) and Thomas Ridley Milburn (1862-1943) (see Plate 44). They were Sunderland's best known and busiest architects in the early years of the century, having gone into partnership in 1897, and produced houses in all parts of the town as well as buildings of such quality as the Fire Station and Law Courts, the Water Company offices and the Empire Theatre. They later worked on theatres in Cardiff and London for Moss Empires. Two of William's sons William and Stanley Wayman eventually entered the practice, Stanley leaving in 1947 and starting his own practice S. W. Milburn & Partners.

The Hat and Feather was rebuilt in 1904, taking the place of the old pub which had had a front bar and select bar with two rear sitting rooms. The new

design was dramatic, using a pair of ogee capped towers and a cupola as eyecatchers on a constricted site just to

44. *William and T. R. Milburn*
(Miss E. Milburn)

the west of and below the parish church. The style might be described as baroque tending to art nouveau (see Col. Plate 2). The exterior is little changed today, and still displays the original owner's name on the side bays. The lower part of the facade is of pink and grey granite, with ionic pilasters carrying decoration including an egg and dart motif and grotesque heads. The upper floor is an attic storey consisting of a pediment holding a window framed by columns (an aedicule), behind which is a hipped slate roof (see Plate 45). The interior has undergone great alteration but on a plan resembling the original, which featured a long, U-shaped bar counter serving select and public bars, which were divided by the wholesale department in the centre; a sitting room was placed at the rear (see Fig. 22). It was an unusual but straightforward plan providing two spacious drinking areas; the total length of the

45. *Hat and Feather (Greens)*

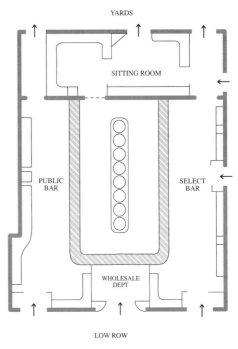

YARDS

SITTING ROOM

PUBLIC
BAR

SELECT
BAR

WHOLESALE
DEPT

LOW ROW

22. *Hat and Feather, 1903 design by
W. and T. R. Milburn;
(from TWA 269/4018-4029 plan 237)*

counter was almost 100ft. (see Plate 46). The pub was taken over by Robert Deuchar about 1915.

Early Edwardian Sunderland was a thriving town, with not only pubs but many other buildings being erected, including theatres, offices and the Alexandra Bridge, begun in 1907. That year, however, saw the beginning of industrial depression

*43. Left: Drawing of Half Moon, High Street
East, Sunderland in 1963 by L. S. Lowry
(SMAG/copyright C.A.Danes)*

for the town, with nine to ten thousand men unemployed by the end of the year and recession in the shipbuilding and other heavy industries continuing during 1908-9. It was the end of a glorious era of pub building, and the war was soon to bring more difficulties for the brewers, already faced with decreased sales. Wartime restrictions on transport hit Vaux particularly hard, their stout trade in Lancashire, Yorkshire and Scotland being severely curtailed. Average national consumption of beer per head had declined from over 30 gallons in 1900-04

*46. Interior of the Hat and Feather before
alteration, August 1972 (SMAG)*

to less than 27 in 1910-14, and many breweries were also in financial trouble because of over-investment in buying public houses. The growth in popularity of working men's clubs, with cheap beer and unregulated opening hours, was another cause of concern for the brewers. Although there was a short post-war boom in demand for beer, consumption was still basically declining, in part because the variety of new leisure activities available to working people - cinema, radio, sports - had broken the pattern of pub attendance. Competition with the background of falling demand resulted in more brewery mergers, with the object of rationalising production rather than increasing available outlets as in the previous bout of mergers.

Vaux were perhaps in a better position with respect to their financial capital in the post-war period than many other brewers, having taken little part in mergers or pub acquisition. This was soon to change, as a new generation of the Vaux family came to control the company. Frank Nicholson, son-in-law of John Story Vaux, joined the company in 1911, and was followed by his son Douglas Nicholson in 1927 and grandson Paul Nicholson in 1965. Vaux began their expansion gradually, taking over J. Heslop's brewery at Stockton-on-Tees for use as a distribution centre in 1923. They followed this in 1925 with a joint effort involving James Calder & Co. of Alloa in the takeover of Robinson Brothers Ltd. of Houghton le Spring, following which the Robinson brewery was closed. In 1927 came the merger which was to establish Vaux as a competitive force in regional brewing, when the now-knighted Sir Frank Nicholson arranged the amalgamation of Vaux and North Eastern Breweries, the new company being registered in July 1927 as Associated

Breweries Ltd.

North Eastern Breweries had become the largest brewery company in Sunderland on its formation in 1896, taking in the local firms Thomas Elwen & Sons and William Story & Co. as well as Bramwells and small breweries from County Durham, Middlesbrough and Burton. The seven founding companies owned 250 public houses between them. There was little expansion for the Breweries in the first two decades of the century, and some contraction in terms of outlets as the licensing justices pursued their policy of closing superfluous pubs; nationally, 3736 pubs were closed between 1906 and 1914. By 1912 the Breweries still owned 26 pubs in Sunderland and the surrounding villages, the same number as Newcastle Breweries owned in that area in 1914; over half the Newcastle Breweries houses were in Monkwearmouth. As with Vaux, North Eastern Breweries began to expand in the 1920s, taking over breweries in Hartlepool and Darlington in 1925.

After amalgamation, Associated Breweries increased the pace of expansion with takeovers in Newcastle, Berwick and Blyth before the Second World War. Having changed their name to Vaux and Associated Breweries Limited in 1940, they ranged further afield and engulfed Lorimer & Clark of Edinburgh in 1946, Steel, Coulson of Edinburgh in 1959, John Wright of Perth in 1961 and S. H. Ward of Sheffield in 1973 amongst others. 1973 saw another change of name to Vaux Breweries Limited, and more takeovers which frequently resulted in brewery closure but expansion of the Vaux empire of outlets, the company owning 789 pubs by 1975. Some of the breweries which survived the 1970s intact were closed by Vaux in the 1980s; the Darley

brewery at Thorne, Yorkshire was shut in 1986 and the Lorimer & Clark brewery in 1987.

The company has survived by a policy of expansion combined with investment in its licensed houses and diversification of trade into the working men's club business, hotels and restaurants. In 1975 they supplied over 1000 clubs and about 4000 free houses, still as important to Vaux as the nineteenth century free trade. Their licensed houses are widespread and are typically vernacular buildings which have been frequently updated, such as the Red Lion at Berwick, transformed in 1988 into Sylvesters (see Plate 47). The pub is one of four listed in Berwick in 1821 when it was the posting house, and stands at the northern end of a stone built terrace in the town's main street. It is a plain Georgian building decorated with a pair of giant pilasters and an ionic columned porch, from whose roof a carving of the red lion has recently been removed to the parapet. The bay window and its excellent stained glass are the result of inter-war improvements. There are several Vaux houses in

47. Red Lion

48. Grotto

minor boom in pub building which occurred between the wars, when classical, neo-Tudor and modernist pubs were erected in the suburbs of Tyneside. Thus the Vaux public house stock is generally nineteenth century, and they have also taken on some peculiar houses, for instance the Lord Crewe Arms in the model village of Blanchland, built by the Earls of Crewe from 1752 onwards to house workers from the lead mines. The pub itself is Georgian but includes part of the Prior's House of Blanchland Abbey, founded in 1165 and dissolved in 1539; one bar occupies the stone vaulted chamber of the Prior's House. Strangest of all the Vaux pubs is the Grotto, on the beach at Marsden Bay in South Shields. The caves at Marsden were first inhabited in 1782, and a house was eventually built on the site which was licensed in the late nineteenth century when the Bay became a tourist attraction. Vaux took on the lease in 1898, bought the Grotto in 1936 and modernised it two years later; an elegant modernist two storey bow window is now the main feature of the pub, while its long open terrace epitomises the 1930s search for sun and space (see Plate 48).

Current Vaux policy on pub modernisation places them in the forefront of the neo-Victorians; their refurbishments combine genuine old fittings with new work to create a lightweight version of the original decorated Victorian pub. Their own Brewery Tap in Dunning Street and the Borough in Vine Place, Sunderland are two of the best examples, both small pubs in which this treatment has been very successful. Sunderland is fortunate in having retained excellent examples of Victorian and Edwardian pub architecture complete with interior fittings, and a brewery which carries out modernisation work with some feeling for the quality

Berwick, and indeed their strength in pub ownership has always lain outside the conurbations of Tyneside and Wearside, in the market towns and mining villages.

Unlike Newcastle, Sunderland did not have the

of material and craft skills. Even if this is largely because it is a profitable policy to follow, their Victorian equivalents would have no doubt agreed on the point. It is ironic but not surprising that as one pub loses its Victorian fittings, another snaps them up; neo- or brewers' Victorian is certainly the style of the late 1980s for the small urban pub.

CHAPTER NINE

Oswald the Architects

THE architectural output of Septimus, Joseph, Harold and Gilbert Oswald spanned the years 1853 to 1945, styles from neo-classical to neo-gothic, buildings from churches to cricket pavilions and towns from Yorkshire to Scotland. The three generations of the Oswald family made their mark on the north east with buildings which were part of the townscape rather than monumental edifices; theirs were the factories, schools, pubs and shops which were the essential stuff of everyday life. The history of the Oswald practice is complex, but the story of their public house work reflects the breadth of styles in which they designed and the variety of clients and contractors involved. Many of their pubs have survived relatively intact and are still performing their original function, and are fitting memorials to a practice which helped shape the north east.

Septimus Oswald was born on 18 October 1824, the seventh son of Gateshead worsted dealer Joseph Oswald whose family had been in business in Newcastle since the early eighteenth century. Septimus was first articled to Newcastle architect and surveyor Andrew Oliver, then appointed as an assistant to Henry Welsh, the county surveyor for Northumberland. He began practising as an architect in 1853, and set up on his own in 1855, working from St Nicholas' Buildings in Newcastle. His work in the 1860s was generally on a small scale, including such buildings as schools, a police station, a chapel and a workhouse in Newcastle and the suburbs, as well as a large housing development at Jarrow. It was at this time that he began working on public houses, an element of the practice which was to grow considerably before the end of the century.

In February 1862 he produced a design for an inn at Jarrow, the client being innkeeper Henry Barrasford. In terms of style, the building could have passed for a typical Victorian villa; it was to be constructed of brick with stone dressings, the corner entrance being emphasised by a pedimented gable and small balcony over a rusticated doorcase. Inside, the customer could enter a small snug from the bar, or venture into the rear parlour; the Oswald pub at this stage was an adapted house design. A firm of South Shields builders, Richardson & Thompson, built the pub for an estimated £530; it was not an extravagant design, as although stone was used for the external dressings, Oswald specified Wilkinson's Artificial Stone for the chimney pieces, an economical substitute

The 1870s saw an expansion of Oswald's work on local housing developments, his designs for villas and terraces being used in Newcastle, Saltwell and Shipcote in Gateshead, and Felling, where he worked for the Felling Coal, Iron and Chemical Company. The pub work continued sporadically, but was clearly not an important part of the practice workload at this time. Septimus' son, Joseph, completed his articles in the practice in 1872, and was taken into partnership by his father in 1876 at the age of 25 (he was born on 19 March 1851). Both father and son became deeply involved with local professional bodies, although they took less interest in public affairs; Septimus was a founder member of the Northern Architectural Association in 1858, becoming its President in 1880, while Joseph was President in 1893 and 1894. Joseph was elected a Fellow of the Royal Institute of British Architects in 1891, and was later a member of the RIBA Council. He was also a keen antiquarian, as his father had been; they both contributed papers to antiquarian journals and for many years Joseph was an officer of the Society of Antiquaries of Newcastle upon Tyne.

The 1880s saw a gradual increase in the amount of time the practice, now known as Septimus Oswald & Son, devoted to public house design, although Joseph was concentrating on building up what was to become a large general practice operating throughout northern England. He laid out the High Gosforth Park race course in 1881 when the races were moved from the Town Moor, and did a similar job for Hexham Steeplechases around 1890. Septimus was forced to retire in 1891 due to ill health, and died on 26 November 1894. Joseph was left to run the practice, which had moved to offices in Mosley Street, and to oversee a dramatic change in the nature of their commissions as the public house rebuilding boom gathered strength.

Joseph Oswald (see Plate 49) rapidly developed his own style for the small late Victorian public house. Its exterior was not at all flamboyant, being in a basic shop front style with large windows separated by pilasters, but the interior was often a different matter, with sturdy Queen Anne style bar fittings set off by frilly Gothic screens. The Albion Inn, on the corner of Albion Road and Nile Street, North Shields, is a good extant example of the basic Joseph Oswald pub. Its exterior (designed in 1892) could now be described as dull, as the pilasters have lost their original tile panels and the parapet is minus its advertising board, but its appearance does give some flavour of the 1890s shop front style. In fact the pub

49. Above: Joseph Oswald, 1851-1930
(Newcastle upon Tyne City Library)

ELEVATION TOWARDS ARGYLE ST^{RT}.

50. Duke of Argyle, 1891 design by Septimus Oswald & Son
(TWA 234/3570)

would have been far more outwardly attractive because of the liberal use of lights and coloured glass, which simultaneously decorated both the inside and outside of the building. Oswald's Duke of Argyle, designed in 1891 for an Argyle Terrace/Argyle Street corner site near what is now Manors Metro Station in Newcastle, had elegantly worked removable glass screens in wooden frames which covered the lower part of each ground floor window (see Plate 50). Their basic design varied little from pub to pub, but the glass usually carried coloured elements relevant either to the name of the pub or the particular room concealed behind the screen. Above the screen and visible from outside the pub would be light fittings, which could be hanging, attached to the screen or mounted on a rail which crossed the architrave of the window. The Blyth and Tyne Hotel (1897, Charlotte Street/Stephenson Street corner, North Shields, now demolished) had an ornate but not atypical gas fitting in which the supports for two lamps curled away from a central column, the whole edifice stretching half the length of the window. The Cumberland Grill, rebuilt in 1893 in East Holborn, the South Shields docklands, was a typical 1890s Oswald pub, with shop front elevation, tiled pilasters and window screens. It was one of the last remaining pubs in East Holborn, outlasted only by the Rose and Crown (still standing) which retains most of its original counter, back bar fitting and embossed windows.

In general the remaining small Victorian pubs, frequently on corner sites, have lost much of their external decoration and often all their internal fittings, and in terms of quality of craft skills are poor things compared with the original versions. Fortunately several Oswald interiors have remained relatively unscathed, and it is still possible to see the rich mix of luxurious materials and unfettered design skills which lay behind the rather mundane exteriors. The average Oswald interior is harder to describe than his exterior work, as he did not keep to a set plan, but it was always highly decorative. It usually comprised a bar, a family department (off sales) and a select room or sitting room near the bar; after this threesome could come the tap room, news room, buffet and commercial room, depending on the size of the pub or hotel. Oswald's 1894 design for the Grey Bull in Oldgate, Morpeth squeezed a tap room into a rear bay window behind the three core rooms, while in contrast the Addison Hotel in Heaton was rebuilt in 1890 and extended in 1896 to finally give the core combination plus a smoke room, buffet and grill room. The site plan, local circumstances and the size of the client's purse would dictate the number of rooms and level of decoration, as well as the quality of materials used.

The screen between the grill room and buffet in the Addison was a magnificent arcade of wooden tracery, one of the most intricate designs produced by the practice in the 1890s (see Plate 51). It was constructed in softwood (American yellow pine was specified) by a Gateshead man, T. Lamb of the General Building Establishment; Oswald rarely brought in contractors from outside the area in which he was working. Specifications were minutely detailed, as were the architect's drawings provided for the contractors; for bar counters, Cuban mahogany was often required, a reddish tan wood with interesting markings. Back bar fittings were French polished mahogany, the finish of which had to be approved by the architect, while less visible parts of the fittings were made of pine (or 'deal').

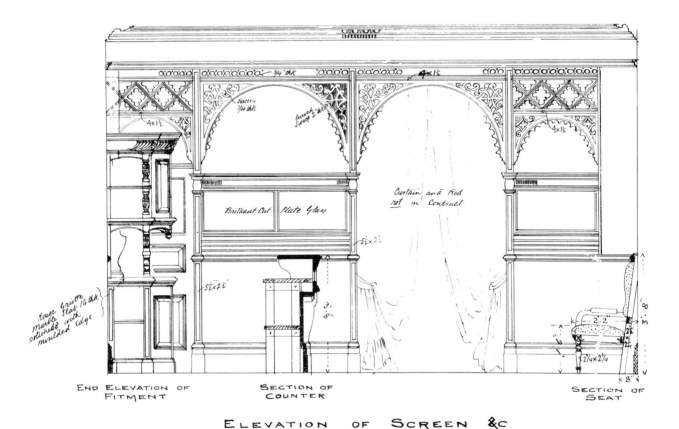

ELEVATION OF SCREEN &c

51. *Addison Hotel, 1896 design for screen by Septimus Oswald & Son (TWA 234/1274)*

The vast variety of glass - silvered, bevelled, embossed and so on - used by the Oswald practice in public house decoration normally came from the Newcastle firm Reed, Millican & Co. of Market Street. For all but the most complex designs, Oswald used a builder from the immediate locality of the pub site and sought tenders for decorative materials from a small range of mainly Newcastle suppliers; the remaining Oswald designs show the high level of local craft skills at the end of the nineteenth century.

Who were the clients for these ornate exhibitions of Victorian interior design? During the early years of the practice they had been innkeepers or small businessmen, but as competition in the

EAST ELEVATION

1. Left: Wolsington House Hotel, Burdon Main
Row, design by J. P. Spencer, 17 May 1901
(NTPD)
2. Above: Hat and Feather, Sunderland, 1903,
by W. and T. R. Milburn
(TWA 269/4018-4029 plan 237)

brewing industry increased in the 1890s, so the clients tended to become brewers or wine and spirit merchants with chains of public houses. Joseph Oswald worked for Morpeth wine and spirit merchants cum brewers Hopper and Anderson (the Grey Bull), Westgate Road brewer Henry Davidson, and Newcastle landowners the Quin Trustees, amongst many others, but his two most important trade clients were George Bell, of wine and spirit merchants Bell & Taylor, and the Newcastle Breweries. The work for the Breweries was just a foretaste of what was to come in the twentieth century, when the practice designed several important 1930s reformed pubs, but the bulk of the Bell or Bell & Taylor pubs were produced in the 1890s or just after the turn of the century.

George Bell was a brewer's agent, born in the Yorkshire village of Ravensworth (just north of Richmond) in 1849. He married a Newcastle woman, Annie Simpson, and they set up home in 1878 at 32 Percy Gardens, Tynemouth, where their son John was born two years later. At that time Percy Gardens was a new and prestigious address; it is a crescent-shaped terrace of three storey houses facing Tynemouth Priory and the sea, the houses being built individually as speculative developments in the 1870s. They have double height bay windows and ornate porches and balconies, and are laden down with decorative elements; the Gardens were undoubtedly the height of fashion on the coast in the late nineteenth century, but today present a rather shabby facade to the sea front. By 1898 the address had become a haven for the drink trade, with James and Alexander Deuchar at 44 and 45 respectively, and spirit merchants William McConnell and David Williamson at 25 and 28. Also living in the Gardens were the Tynemouth Town Clerk and assorted merchants, accountants, ship owners and the like, making the crescent a pocket of local influence.

George Bell built up his agency business during the 1880s and diversified into innkeeping from the early 1890s, one of his first commissions for the Oswald practice being the Duke of Argyle in 1891. His base was the Berwick Arms in North Shields (Coach Lane/Trinity Street corner), and its magnificent faience facade is described in detail in Chapter 10. Within ten years he was in control of pubs in Newcastle, North Shields and South Shields, Hartlepool and Durham, and had gone into partnership with Henry Taylor of Low Fell as wine

and spirit merchants Bell & Taylor. They ran the North Shields part of their business (where they were also beer bottlers) from the Victoria Hotel in William Street, and by 1901 held seven pubs in the town, including the Albion, the Blyth and Tyne and the Railway Hotel (now an amusement arcade on Nile Street, next to North Shields Metro Station). The rebuilt Cumberland Grill in South Shields was also a Bell & Taylor establishment.

George Bell moved from Tynemouth to Gosforth in 1902 and the business began to decline slightly, although his company continued to provide commissions for the Oswald practice well into the 1900s. Bell died around 1920, and although the firm Bell & Taylor continued in existence at the Berwick Arms until 1929, their main period of influence on public house design in North Shields was the 1900s. In Newcastle, the Vine Inn (see Chapter 1), close to the firm's city headquarters in the Bigg Market, showed what a decorative extravaganza the Oswald/Bell & Taylor combination could produce for a prime site.

The typical pub commission given to the Oswald practice by Bell & Taylor was the rebuilding on a similar scale of a small pub, usually comprising a bright new facade, a rearrangement of the internal accommodation and a high level of interior decorative work. Although Newcastle Breweries did their share of small-scale rebuilding work, their commissions to the Oswald practice in the 1890s were for very large houses which replaced small city pubs, reflecting their dominant position in the local urban licensed trade. The Wheat Sheaf Hotel (1897-98) and the Blue Bell Hotel (1900-1) both on Roker Avenue in Monkwearmouth, Sunderland were two such cases, the much-redesigned Blue Bell finally emerging as a piece of turreted Edwardian baroque. The old Wheat Sheaf, run under the Swinburne name, was a three storey corner pub with an ordinary shop-front style ground floor situated on the road leading north from Wearmouth Bridge. The Breweries wanted to make the most of such a busy site, and the new design was for a grand neo-classical stone-faced building sweeping round the curve of the corner, decorated with a giant order of ionic pilasters and with the name of the pub carved on the frieze (see Plate 52). It even had a Greek Key or fret pattern frieze just above the ground floor windows, but its most elegant decorative feature was a carved wheat sheaf in a cartouche above the main entrance. The interior was lit at first by a combination of gas and electricity, the gas lamps being mostly reserved for the large corner bar where they were mounted on double brackets rising from columns behind the bar counter.

The Wheat Sheaf typified the turn of the century public house work of the Oswald practice, being a striking design for a local client which was built by a local contractor, in this case builder John Stott of Southwick Road, only yards from the site of the pub. Joseph Oswald's son Harold had become a partner in 1899, although the practice was still known as Septimus Oswald & Son up to 1900, when it finally became Joseph Oswald & Son; this remained its title until it ceased to function in 1969. The facades produced by the practice in the 1900s were visually stunning and hid a slight change of decorative style for the interiors, which took the Queen Anne style to its opulent limits. Their interiors were designed as thoroughly as the facades, with details drawn and materials specified down to the last seat cushion and

52. Wheat Sheaf Hotel, Roker Avenue, Monkwearmouth

table top.

Harold Oswald may have been responsible for the increased use of colourful materials in the work of the practice, as although glazed architectural faience was available in the 1890s, Joseph Oswald had used only the occasional panel of tiles on a pilaster or doorcase in his designs. By 1904, Joseph and Harold were collaborating on the design for the Central Arcade in Newcastle's Exchange Buildings, next to the Monument. The building was being remodelled following a fire, and the Oswald design suggested facing the entire arcade in Burmantofts

faience. The result was a great success, and the faience, in shades of brown and yellow, still looks in excellent condition. This colourful work was followed by Joseph Oswald's Haymarket Office building for Newcastle Breweries, which was begun in 1901. (It is now the home of the University School of Education.) The entrance hall, clerks' and accountants' room and an upper corridor were all faced in glazed faience, this time in turquoise, buff and pale yellow (see Col. Plate 3). The plaque and fire surrounds showing the Breweries' name or logo were made especially for the new offices, which were luxuriously fitted out (see Col. Plate 4).

The glazed faience found its way on to the pub facades in the 1900s, Bell & Taylor's Railway Hotel in North Shields being a typical example of its use. The pub had been altered by the Joseph Oswald in 1894 and a buffet added in 1897, but the shining facade in shades of golden brown did not appear until 1910. This type of work was not done locally; the practice produced a detailed drawing of the design required, which was then sent to a Leeds firm, probably the Leeds Fireclay Company at their Burmantofts works. This contract drawing was returned to the architects in 1910 and the faience would have arrived from Leeds soon afterwards; it was then attached to the stonework of the Hotel by a system of metal bolts and pins. 78 years later it looks almost as good as new, and only the frieze containing the name of the Hotel has been obscured.

Some of the interior designs produced by the Oswald practice during the 1900s were superlative, and one of their finest examples remains in full use and largely intact today, at the Half Moon in New Elvet, Durham. The facade and front bar date from 1894, when Messrs. Mackay & Co. asked Joseph

3. Top left: Entrance hall of Haymarket Offices, Newcastle Breweries, Joseph Oswald & Son, 1901 onwards
4. Bottom left: Fire surround in Haymarket Offices, Newcastle Breweries
5. Above: Back bar fitting in buffet, Half Moon, New Elvet, Durham, Joseph Oswald & Son, 1908-9

Oswald to prepare a design for rebuilding the pub. The facade is in his unexceptional shop front style, with delicate red floral tile panels on the pilasters, and behind it were three bars served by a single L-shaped bar counter and separated by screens. By 1908 George Bell had taken over the pub, when he proposed the addition of a rear buffet. The Oswald design extended the bar counter in a semicircle to form the buffet bar, and opened out the front bars by removing most of the screens. The buffet fittings were produced by Seymour Nelson, a Durham joiner and undertaker, and include the spectacular semicircular mahogany bar counter, a solidly Queen Anne back bar fitting (without the central clock which appeared in the original design), and a fire surround (see Col. Plate 5). The designs for seats, tables, fire surrounds, wallpaper and glass were all specified by the architects - a total drinking environment.

The Oswald practice continued to thrive throughout the 1900s, when its office moved to Worswick Chambers in Worswick Street, Newcastle, but the war years and the 1920s were less profitable in terms of commissions for all types of work. Public house work decreased as the brewers came under pressure from both the temperance movement and falling beer consumption, and there was to be no repetition of the glorious turn of the century designs. Joseph Oswald became ill in the early 1920s, and although he did not retire from practice, Harold was effectively in charge. On 14 January 1930 Joseph Oswald died at his home in Jesmond; he had been Newcastle's oldest architect at the age of 78. The Oswald practice carried on with Harold's brother Gilbert now involved, and again moved its office, this time to Bradburn House, Northumberland Street. After Harold's death in about 1937 Gilbert was the last of the family to be connected with the practice; Gilbert Oswald died in 1945, but the practice survived for another 24 years, moving to Archbold Terrace in 1955.

Their public house work did not cease completely after the early twentieth century boom,

53. Duke of Wellington

as a small resurgence took place in the 1930s when Newcastle Breweries commissioned a series of reformed pubs from the practice. There were two basic styles: for the early 1930s, red brick and pilasters as in the Percy Arms, Front Street, Tynemouth (see Chapter 4) and for the later 1930s, a rambling neo-Georgian with occasional classical ornamentation, typified by the Green Tree (1939) in Ferguson's Lane, Benwell or the Foxhunters outside Whitley Bay. The Duke of Wellington (1934) in Kenton Lane, Gosforth is the archetypal thirties suburban pub, a two storey stuccoed neo-Georgian box with brick imitation quoins, situated close to a busy juction on a main road (see Plate 53). Unusually, some of the internal wooden panelling in the Duke of Wellington is still intact.

In terms of their public house work, the overall contribution of the Oswald practice to the Tyneside townscape rests mainly with the highly decorated pubs of the 1900s, for which Harold Oswald may largely be held responsible. North Shields in particular has a surprising array of pubs with faience facades, although their interiors cannot compete with those of the city pubs. On grounds of size alone, the 1930s pubs are the most obvious reminders of the work of the practice, but their interiors have been much changed. The range of pub styles produced by the practice in the nineteenth and twentieth centuries shows the Oswalds to have been eclectic designers, well versed in giving the client a building which would attract customers. They followed the same principles as other pub designers, using lights and coloured or reflecting materials to sumptuous effect, but the standard of design and craftwork was particularly high in their pubs; their clients, most importantly George Bell, must have found the increased outlay commercially viable. Apart from their public house work, the Oswalds produced a great many other buildings throughout the north east in the 90 years in which they were connected with the practice bearing their name. It was a practice of regional rather than local importance, and pubs were only a small part of its work, but a part which was carried out with great attention to detail and sometimes inspired specification. Their designs were not revolutionary, but were of the highest quality, and it is a tribute to their skill that so many of their pubs have survived and perform their original function.

CHAPTER TEN

Terracotta and Tiles

The Decorated Pub

THE Victorian and Edwardian public house was a sensual beast, its prime aim the attraction of customers from the murky streets without to the lights, colours, rich materials and glittering surfaces within. The prospective drinker was initially tempted from afar by the picturesque outline of the building, a corner tower topped by a dome or gables swirling high above street level. Closer to the pub, the walls glowed with colour from tiles and faience, and its identity became apparent - a carved stag looked down on the entrance, tile pictures of swans floated around the outer walls - and twinkling lights illuminated the bright glass screens just inside the windows. Once over the threshold, the customer was in a world of highly polished surfaces, glass, wood and metal, all reflecting the colours of fabrics, tiles, bottles, glasses and people; these were not ordinary buildings, but buildings designed to tease the senses.

They were not, though, built for fun but with a serious commercial intent, the extraction of money from the drinking masses. In this they proved very successful until the fickle public, offered more leisure time and more choice in the way of entertainment,

decided that the novelty had worn off the spectacular pub and opted for other pastimes. This search for new stimuli combined with local economic circumstances to produce clear variations in the number of highly decorated pubs, particularly in Tyne and Wear. The Sunderland industrial boom ended in 1907, and with it most pub building, but North Shields today has a glorious collection of pubs faced in brightly coloured faience, most of which were built or rebuilt around 1910-1914, when the local fishing industry was at its peak.

For an architect, a commission to design a new pub at the turn of the century meant an opportunity to indulge in experiments with colours and materials, the process being made easier by the firms whose business it was to offer ready-made solutions to the problems of decorating pubs; the architect could choose from catalogues of tile manufacturers or allow faience makers to fill in the details of a design. Although brightly coloured buildings may appear somehow foreign to the English architectural scene, this is a misreading of history, as the English love of decoration, both on facades and internal, has been apparent since Anglo- Saxon times. It was initially most obvious in the religious context, with Anglo-Saxon cross carvings, Romanesque mural paintings, and the increasingly complex decorative forms of the Gothic cathedrals reflecting the power of the church and its ability to pay for such work. The great Elizabethan and Jacobean country houses followed, overflowing with decoration inside and out, their real inheritors being perhaps not the houses built in cooler Georgian styles but the gratuitously picturesque Victorian piles. By the nineteenth century power lay with commerce as well as Crown and church, and the new buildings of trade and industry exhibited their functions but retained some decorative elements, the decoration itself being functional in the case of shops or pubs. Although the twentieth century modern movement in architecture was a reaction against overblown decoration and non-functional forms, pubs built in this style are often more attractive than other buildings of the era, because of the specific needs of the building type (expansive windows, luxurious fittings) and the continued use of high quality materials. New pubs are still in a transitional phase, the urban harshness of the 1960s having been replaced by twee brick vernacular, but the resurgence of craft skills could lead to a modern equivalent of the decorated pub, rather than the recent but undoubtedly popular pastiche versions.

The turn of the century public house is the true inheritor of the tradition of brightly coloured buildings begun by those Greek temples which so impressed Britain's architects in the early nineteenth century. C. R. Cockerell in particular, the architect of Oxford's Ashmolean Museum (1841-5), had travelled extensively in Greece, and attempted to translate not only Greek motifs but Greek use of external colour into his English buildings. The Ashmolean design uses stonework of contrasting colours, but the dampness of the English climate meant that external painted colouration would rapidly decay, and thus it is largely the motifs rather than the colours of Greek architecture which have had most impact on English architectural style. Later Victorian architects took to polychromatic brickwork as an expression of delight in colourful forms, a trend originating with John Ruskin's work on the Gothic buildings of Venice, but this High Victorian enthusiasm had diminished by the time of the pub building boom. When mass produced glazed ceramics became available towards the turn of the century, these brightly coloured and durable materials were rarely used externally except on entertainment buildings; the Greek temple had been forgotten. Between the 1880s and about 1910 the easily cleaned, hygienic glazed tile appeared inside all types of public buildings as well as the halls, hearths and kitchens of houses. Apart from their use in public houses, shops and the occasional theatre, external ceramics were a rarity; Halsey Ricardo's North Kensington house (1905-7) was exceptional, with its blue and green glazed bricks, as was the Everard's factory (1900) in Bristol, with its entirely ceramic facade. More usually, a coloured building in an Edwardian street would be a pub: in London, perhaps a combination of carved stonework, elaborate gables and red brick; in Birmingham, the buff, brown and red hues of terrcotta; on the north bank of the Tyne, from Walker to North Shields, shades of yellow, green and brown faience were the norm. The small town pub used bright colour as its most immediately attractive external feature in place of the imposing height, towers and gables of the big city pub.

To look more closely at the use of decoration in and on the Northumbrian pub, it will be helpful to consider each element of the design separately, from the elevation as a whole through the facade and its materials via iron and glasswork to the interior. The 1920s and 1930s reformed pubs too have distinct, and distinctly different, styles from the Victorian and Edwardian pubs, which resulted from new sets of social and architectural pressures on both brewers and architects.

THE ELEVATION

Several city pubs have already been described which have the archetypal design of a tall corner tower or dome dominating a narrow street, including the Bee Hive in Newcastle's Cloth Market (see Chapter 1) and the collection of domed pubs in Felling (see Chapter 5), but the area is rich in examples of this style. The Scotia in Mile End Road, South Shields is one of the best, standing at an important crossroads which it marks with a magnificent corner tower topped by an art nouveau turret cap with a wrought iron fleche (see Plate 54). The Edwardian baroque pub (listed grade II) was built in 1903-4 for Alexander Deuchar's company by local architect Henry Grieves, who also built several villas in Westoe village.

The now-demolished Duke of Cumberland, on the south side of Newcastle's Scotswood Road at its junction with Hare Street, was rebuilt in 1900-01 by South Shields architect J. Wardle Donald, who emphasised the acute angle of the corner site with a two storey circular tower which rose from the pub's

54. Scotia.

roof between the dormer windows and the chimney-stacks. The top floor of the tower was a single circular room with windows around most of its circumference, which was itself contained in an open columned drum; the dome was capped by a fleche, and the whole composition made up one of the most spectacular pubs along a road renowned for them.

The tower of the Lamb's Arms in West Ryton is more an Arts and Crafts affair, being a two decker corner oriel having several design points in common with the Royal Turf in Felling. The resemblance is

55. Punch Bowl, 1877 design by John Gibson
(TWA T186/8292)

explained by the fact that architect B. F. Simpson produced both pubs for Robert Deuchar around 1899, although the Lamb's Arms with its three stories and decorative half-timbering was a much more costly building in terms of the architect's fee. Apart from its tower, the Lamb's Arms also has windows of excellent brilliant cut glass with art nouveau leaded top lights, and a terracotta dragon guarding the end of the roof ridge.

Corner towers were not only a late Victorian/Edwardian notion; the Punch Bowl on Jesmond Road, Jesmond was built in 1878 to a design by local architect John Gibson for wine and spirit merchant Farquhar Laing. Gibson's idiosyncratic combination of Scottish Baronial, Gothic and French Renaissance - Tyneside Baronial? - shown in his elegant line drawing was built almost as designed, the main alteration being the siting of the shop front window on the side elevation (see Plate 55). The tower is a Renaissance stump decorated with ironwork, and although not as brash as the Edwardian corner towers has the same intent, the attraction of customers towards the corner entrance.

The tower was used to great effect by Cackett and Burns Dick in their 1901 design for the Bridge Hotel, Castle Garth, Newcastle (see Plate 56). The work was commissioned by John Fitzgerald, and although the lower stories have many interesting features, the slightly formal Edwardian building breaks out into a wildly baroque square tower on its fourth storey. It carries art nouveau swags and a decorative cap as well as the owner's name; altogether a most unusual design seen at its best from the north bound train.

The Bridge Hotel has a peculiar site, opposite the Castle and tucked into the lee of the High Level Bridge, one in which a building can be easily ignored unless it has a clear identity. City pubs without corner sites share this problem, which some overcome by sheer size and others with unusual materials or picturesque design. The Bay Horse Hotel in Bishop Auckland's busy Newgate Street announces itself as a pub with a large third storey gable projecting over the street, the whole design being in a gentle neo-Georgian style with two triangular oriel windows. Looking even less like a shop is the Coach and Horses in Wallsend High Street, which might only be mistaken for the neighbouring old Town Hall. It is a large red brick building (the High Street elevation has 11 bays) in the neo-Jacobean style, with stone dressings including urns on the parapet and cherubic carvings, and tall ribbed chimney-stacks. It was built for W. B. Reid in 1902 by their company architect Watson, and dominates its site by means of size alone.

Smaller town and city pubs often have picturesque detailing which differentiates them from nearby buildings. The Foresters Arms in Ryhope Street, Ryhope has a series of dumpy, swagged ionic

56. *Bridge Hotel*

columns which act as window mullions and slightly ludicrous doorcases decorated with scrolls, swags and hearts. In Sunderland, the cornice of the Kings Arms in Farringdon Row is marked by giant wooden ball finials, while in South Shields a carved stag's head complete with antlers stares down from the gable of the eponymous pub in Fowler Street. The Stags Head, built in 1897, was a Bell & Taylor pub by 1914 and is now a Bass house. The Grapes in St Mary's Chare, Hexham has a pair of badly weathered shaped stone gables informing potential customers of the name of the pub and its date of building, 1899. A good pub architect could use the various decorative elements available to simultaneously enhance the attractiveness of the building, tell the potential customer its name and create an identity for the pub by using figurative carving, giving dates or brewers' names or including generalised symbols like the sunflower to indicate that the building was the height of aesthetic fashion. The architect could also take a more commonplace element of the design, such as the bay window, and extend it until it became a decorative feature, as in the Black Bulls of both High Street, Wooler (an oriel) and Bridge Street, Morpeth where the bow window projects the pub on to the street.

The picturesque elevation can also occur in buildings not originally designed as pubs, the best north eastern example being the castellated Mitre off Benwell Lane in Benwell, Newcastle. It began life as Benwell Tower, a country house designed for Thomas Crawhall in 1830 by John Dobson, the Newcastle architect; the output of Dobson's vast practice included over 100 country houses and over 50 churches, largely in Northumbria, his best known work being Newcastle Central Station (1846-50). At Benwell Tower he produced an asymmetrical, Gothic extension to the remains of an old mansion, and it is this more recent part of the building which is now the Mitre, so called because the Tower was presented to the Bishopric of Newcastle in 1881 for use as the Bishop's Palace. In the 1950s and 1960s it was the headquarters of the Fire Brigade before standing empty until Whitbread bought it in 1982 and turned it into a pub, which they sold in 1986. The fabric of the building has survived these changes

remarkably well; the old dining room and morning room are now used as bars, and the drawing room, still with some vestige of its once splendid view over the Tyne and Derwent valleys, has become the pool room. The most impressive of the rooms, most of which have high, heavily ribbed ceilings, dark stained oak panelling and fine decorative fire surrounds, are the library with its carved shelving and the chapel, added when the Tower was the Bishop's Palace and incongruously used for rock concerts in the early 1980s.

The Border Minstrel in High Gosforth Park, at the Newcastle race course is another pub made from a country house, in this case a side pavilion of Gosforth House which was built in 1755-64 by James Paine for the M.P. Charles Brandling. Paine was a great country house designer who often worked in northern England (including periods at both Raby Castle, Co. Durham and Alnwick Castle), but the conversion of Gosforth House into part of the race course grandstand in 1880 and its gutting by fire in 1914 (internal reconstruction 1921) has left the pub and its surroundings with little of its original character.

A contrasting but wildly picturesque pub is the Tan Hill Inn at Tan Hill, the farthest tip of south west Co. Durham only half a mile from the point at which the Durham, Cumbrian and Yorkshire borders meet. It is a house in the country though not a country house, vernacular architecture not 'great architecture', and the epitome of rural romanticism perched on the bleak moors 1732 feet above sea level. It was built where the old pack-horse trails crossed, using coursed rubble stone and slates, with dressed stone architraves and large quoins on the single storey porch. Also deep in the remote south

Durham moors is Allenheads, on the River East
Allen, where the Old Inn is now being used as a
heritage centre. This old village inn was run by
Thomas Dawson and his wife Mary in 1841, their six
children and three servants sharing the pub which is
a typical Weardale stone building with its own free-
standing bread oven. Mary Dawson had taken over
as innkeeper by 1851 and continued to run the inn
until the 1870s, when her son Thomas took charge;
the family were still in residence in 1881, Mary by
then being aged 78, but the inn closed soon
afterwards. The family rented the inn from the
Blackett-Beaumont Company, which had built the
village of Allenheads in order to exploit the lead
ores in the surrounding dales; the Old Inn closed as
the British lead mining industry was beginning to
decline, when foreign mines began producing at a
significantly lower cost.

The rural pub is generally a vernacular building,
picturesque by accident of situation rather than part
of an intentional attempt to attract customers. Its
town and city counterpart, the small corner pub at
the end of a terrace, would be similarly
indistinguishable from the neighbouring houses but
for the brewers' ability to buy eye-catching materials
or objects with which to adorn its facade. A facade
could be covered in coloured faience, decorated by
stone plaques or leafy scrolls of ironwork, or lit by
giant lamps hanging over the entrances. These
decorative tricks were used on pubs large and small,
but in Northumbria, the brightest and best of the
faience work was reserved for smaller pubs,
particularly those of the Tyneside towns to the east
of the great conurbation.

THE DECORATED FACADE

Faience is an umbrella term for a variety of ceramic
materials, all of which consist of types of clay mixed
with various other substances, sometimes glazed, and
then fired at different temperatures. Terracotta is the
unglazed version of faience often used for
ornamenting buildings in the nineteenth century,
which when fired has colours ranging from grey and
buff through the reds to brown. Its basic raw
materials were the shales and fireclays of the Coal
Measures, which were mixed with purer clays to
produce a more attractive colouring. Terracotta slabs
were produced by pressing the mixed raw clay
mixture into plaster moulds, made to a larger size
than the final measurements required to allow for
shrinkage. The moulds were then dried, which
accelerated the shrinkage of the terracotta away from
the mould, thus facilitating its removal. After further
drying, the terracotta slabs were fired at about
1200°C, the kiln being allowed to cool gently to a
low temperature before being unloaded.

The brightly coloured glazed faience blocks used
on pub facades went through a similar process, but
the body of the clay had to be suitable for carrying a
glaze; the white earthenware used for tiles or the
fireclay which produced buff terracotta were both
acceptable. Glazing originally required a second
firing, but in 1888 a single-fired faience was
introduced; the faience could also be relief modelled
resulting in complex decorative pieces. As with the
Railway Hotel in North Shields (see Chapter 9), an
architect requiring a faience facade would send a
contract drawing to the manufacturers, whose
draughtsman would then develop a detailed drawing
and have it approved by the architect. The faience

was then produced block by block, and for major buildings was assembled in the factory to check that all the blocks fitted together; the blocks were then numbered before delivery. The whole process was time-consuming and expensive for the manufacturers, but architectural ceramics were sometimes regarded as a prestigious loss leader and low quotations were given in order to maintain a high level of production.

Although there were a large number of small firms producing terracotta in the Newcastle area in the mid-nineteenth century, they were never very significant as national producers, possibly because the local market at that time was too small, or at the time when coloured facades became popular they may have lacked a local source of the clays which would carry glaze. Certainly terracotta is not as evident as a building material on the pubs of the north east as it is on those of Birmingham. There is proof that at least one of the faience facades of Tyneside (the Railway Hotel) was produced in Leeds, and it is probable that several others originated at the Burmantoft works of the Leeds Fireclay Company. The company was formed in 1889 when the Burmantofts Pottery, begun in 1842, amalgamated with other fireclay works in the Leeds area. Under the trade name 'Burmantofts' it produced a wide range of tiles and faience, faience production continuing until the works closed in 1957.

By the start of the First World War there were at least seven pubs in North Shields faced entirely in glazed faience, the best of them being the Bell & Taylor Berwick Arms. It had been rebuilt by the Oswald practice in 1891 and altered again in 1900, but the shining yellow, green and brown faience was not added until about 1913 (see Col. Plate 6). The corner porch is notable, as are the yellow dragon heads worked into the floral decoration of the spandrels (see Col. Plate 7). The facade was even more impressive in its original form, when the blank window in the upper floor was filled by a coloured faience plaque advertising Bell & Taylor (see Plate 57); this plaque may still remain under the present boarding.

More usually, the North Shields facades were glazed in shades of brown, varying from a golden brown to a deep ruddy hue, with relief decoration which often included versions of neo-Classical

57. Berwick Arms, North Shields in c1960
(J.C. Lane;NSLSC ACC 2053)

6. *Top left: Berwick Arms*
7. *Bottom left: Berwick Arms,*
detail of faience
8. *Above: Duke of Wellington*

motifs such as ionic pilasters carrying egg and dart moulding. Crane House (the Chain Locker) on New Quay fits this pattern, but it is impossible to say whether the facade was part of its 1905 rebuilding by the Oswald practice or was added a few years later; probably the former. The Railway Hotel facade, another Oswald design in plain brown, dates from 1910-11, while the Tynemouth Lodge on Tynemouth Road (c1914) is a mixture of gold and brown slabs with the pub's name on a yellow background, a common combination. Its facade is gently Georgian in style, particularly the doorcase with its golden swags, and although the basic colour on these faience pubs was similar each design was slightly different. The Crown and Sceptre (Stephenson Street, c1914, demolished) had a yellow and brown faience facade with columns in place of window mullions, and the same materials

were used for the elegant Borough Arms (Gardner Street, 1913, demolished), the faience facade curving gracefully around its acutely angled corner site. The Borough Arms facade was probably produced for brewer W. B. Reid by architect F. R. N. Haswell, who carried out other alterations to the pub and was often given commissions by the company for work in the Tynemouth/North Shields area around the turn of the century.

The Garrick's Head (Saville Street, now Savilles) designed in 1898 by Haswell for W. B. Reid is a much earlier example of a yellow and brown faience facade, used in an unusual combination with brown glazed bricks below ground floor window level. The best glazed brick facade on Tyneside is that of the Royal Hotel in White Street, Low Walker, opposite the Neptune shipyard which became part of Swan Hunter in 1903. Here, glazed brick in yellow and pale brown covers both storeys of the pub.

At least two architectural practices, Haswell and

9. *County Hotel*

Oswald, and three brewers or wine and spirit merchants (Bell & Taylor, Newcastle Breweries, W. B. Reid) were involved in the expensive business of presenting prospective customers in North Shields with attractive, brightly coloured public houses. At a time of local prosperity in both the shipbuilding and fishing industries, the high initial outlay could be recouped relatively quickly; most of the faience facade pubs were located close to the shipyards or docks, so as to be first in line for the workmen's custom. Beside its bright colours, faience also had the advantage of being extremely hard wearing and incurring few maintenance costs, thus it was an ideal material for facing pubs in the hostile seaside environment.

The greatest concentration of faience facades was and still is in North Shields, but some excellent specimens can be found further west. The Duke of Wellington, sited near the river on Northumberland Dock Road beside the Tyne Tunnel entrance at Howdon, is a prime example of the yellow and brown faience style with slight classical overtones (see Col. Plate 8). The severity of the facade is broken only by a few decorative scrolls on the frieze. Inside, the panelled bar counter and part of the high bar fitting running above the counter have survived, and although the original two bars have been made into a single long bar, the pub remains much as it was originally built. Most surprising of all is the County Hotel, on the corner of Walker Road and Brampton Avenue in St Anthony's, again only a quarter mile from the river. The original and unexceptional building was by B. F. Simpson but its present appearance is due to architects T. K. White and S. J. Stephenson of Newcastle, who redesigned the pub for its owner, grocer J. H. Brannen, in May

1906. They specified a faience facade approximating to the design as built, but the suppliers of the faience are unknown. Although the facade is in yellow, green and brown the style is rather more ornate than the North Shields pubs, with cartouches and panels of yellow and green tiles (see Col. Plate 9). The bar counter remains intact, simple but good quality, as well as the upper part of the back fitting.

The most spectacular of the local faience pubs lies south of the river in Albert Street, Hebburn. The Albert is a listed grade II building, although nothing is left of its interior. It was built by J. W. Wardle of South Shields for Gateshead brewer John Rowell & Son Ltd. in 1908, its baroque gold and brown faience featuring cartouches, swags, swirling chamfered corner panels and heavy, classically inspired doorcases (see Col. Plate 10). There are also buff terracotta chimney-stacks, but the upper storey is utterly plain in comparison with the riotous colour below.

Examples of faience facades do exist in the cities, but although they may be of good quality, they are few in number. This is because the city pubs were mainly rebuilt in the 1890s, before the use of glazed faience became fashionable in the north east. Also, narrow city streets tend to diminish the impact of coloured facades, as with the otherwise excellent faience work on the Bee Hive in Cloth Market (Oswald for Newcastle Breweries, 1902). The Rose and Crown on Newcastle's Newgate Street has a blue faience facade including a fine bow window and a pair of lion's heads, but more interesting is the inscription 'D & D' in mosaic on the floor of the recessed doorway. This referred to brewers Duncan & Daglish who commissioned the refacing from Simpson & Lawson in 1914. The best of the

Newcastle faience facades is to be found in Gosforth High Street at the Gosforth Hotel, where Simpson and Lawson again used blue faience in their 1913 refacing for Arrols. The original plans indicate that the architects specified the heavy classical style including the cartouche over the corner door, but whether the snarling animal head above it was designed by architect or manufacturer's draughtsman, it is impossible to say (see Col. Plate 11).

Further afield, the Tram Car Inn on the Green in Southwick, Sunderland was extended in 1906 by Hugh Hedley (architect of Sunderland's Londonderry Hotel) and faced with a delicate yellow and brown combination of faience slabs which included highly decorated doorcases and spandrels. In the Horse Market, Darlington, the Hole in the Wall boasts a light and dark brown faience facade with a central attached ionic column and other classical touches. It was built in 1903-4 for John Smith's Tadcaster Brewery Co., and designed by Harrogate architect George Cooper.

One particular form of faience which achieved greater popularity in the cities was the matt white version which Burmantofts marketed from 1889 as 'Marmo'. Some architects preferred it to the light-reflecting surface of glazed faience which could alter the whole character of a building, and it was much in vogue during the early twentieth century, being used on offices, factories, shops and pubs. It was tremendously hard-wearing and was often used to cover all the external surfaces of a building, including door frames and cornices. Marmo became one of the main Burmantofts products after the First World War, and this type of facing, complete with neo-classical motifs, can be seen on the Burton

House in Croft Street, Newcastle.

The scarcity of faience facades away from the Tyne is paralleled by the lack of terracotta pubs in the region, and the sparse external use of decorative tiles. Wallsend's Duke of York (High Street West) is a bulky three storey essay in neo-classical red terracotta and red brick, and the Cross House Hotel (renovated in late 1988) in Cross Street, Gateshead is a 1902 design in red and white terracotta with a corner tower; neither of these pubs would be out of place in London or Birmingham. Possibly on grounds of cost, brick with terracotta dressing was the norm for local pub rebuilding around the turn of the century; terracotta slabs rarely made up the bulk of the facade. The Rose Inn, Rosehill, Wallsend is a good example of the use of red terracotta dressings including rusticated quoins, cornice and ionic columns/mullions.

Faience was overwhelmingly more popular than tiling for external use on pub facades in the north east, tiles usually being confined to recessed doorways as at the Stags Head in South Shields. The Black Swan in Parkgate, Darlington is the great exception to this general rule, with a dark green glazed brick facade incorporating five superb tile panels, each portraying a black swan. Three different swan designs swim around the facade, and the tilework is complemented by excellent embossed glass windows which also carry the black swan (see Col. Plates 12 and 13). The interior too is well preserved, with a fine back bar fitting.

Few of the great lamps which lit up the facades of the Victorian and Edwardian pubs have survived into the late twentieth century, and in the north east only the Britannia (1896 by J. Wardle Donald) in Westoe Road, South Shields can now give us any

10. Right: Albert
11. Above: Gosforth Hotel

real indication of how dominant this style of lighting could be. The single lamp on its scrolled wrought iron bracket is the most eye-catching feature of this three storey red brick and sandstone pub. Once again, this old idea is being copied on some newly refurbished city pubs, where a row of large and glistening lamps is to be seen hanging above the ground floor facade. More difficult, now, for the great lamps to stand out, as they must compete with shop windows and street lighting, but they will doubtless enhance the 'Victorian' character of the pubs they adorn.

THE GLASS

Not only could the architecture of a Victorian or Edwardian pub enable it to stand out at a distance, its detailed ornamentation could give it a distinct identity in the eyes of prospective drinkers before they had crossed the threshold. The name of the pub would appear on a painted sign board, also perhaps in some form of witty sculpted figure woven into the facade of the building, and almost certainly in the embossed glass of the windows, again perhaps represented pictorially. Other forms of decorative glasswork were used to maintain and strengthen the heady atmosphere of the pub interior, by adding colour and reflections or portraying symbols connected with drinking. The upper lights of windows occasionally carried leaded panels of stained glass, which might show ale or food being served to customers, although they more frequently

contained abstract art nouveau patterns. Small panels of painted glass featuring the pub name were set in stained glass surrounds and could be used for windows or fanlights. By the end of the nineteenth century almost all the windows, mirrors and screens in the typical pub were decorated, the specific design often relating to a single pub.

Much of this glasswork has disappeared from north eastern pubs, but on the evidence remaining it seems likely that there was no local equivalent of the fabulous outbreak of embossing, brilliant cutting, and mirror painting and gilding which occurred in London pub interiors in the 1890s. Embossed glass was originally produced by burning a pattern into the glass with acid and then grinding the remaining raised or embossed area to obscure it and so bring out the transparent pattern. This technique was only capable of giving two tones, the contrast between clear and obscure glass, but French embossing, first used in England in the late 1880s, could give three or more tones by using a series of applications of acid. It could also be used on sheet glass as well as the more expensive plate, thus reducing the price of pub decoration. Brilliant cutting of glass had been available from 1850, but became popular in the 1890s as a means of giving extra sparkle to glass; it involved cutting a pattern into the glass and then polishing the cut surfaces, and could only be carried out on plate glass. The intensity of competition and the amount of money available in the 1890s building boom accounts for the widespread use of all types of decorated glass in late Victorian London pubs, and it is probable that these expensive processes were used in the north east only when conditions were relatively prosperous and pubs were being rebuilt, for example in North Shields just before the First World War.

Certainly two of the best specimens of embossed glass windows were to be seen in the faience pubs of North Shields, at Crane House and the Railway, but sadly the glass of both has long gone. At Crane House, the central design was of a dockside crane, while an express train steamed across the windows of the Railway. The Railway Hotel, Durham Road, Birtley has retained part of its original glass, which decorates a delightful brown faience facade with ionic columns, a recessed doorway and a niche. The glass, which curves gently round to the recessed entrance, shows the inevitable steam train (see Col. Plate 14). Ships are the theme of the fine windows at the Ship in the Hole (previously the Ship Inn), Gainers Terrace, Wallsend, where the embossed glass features sailing and steam ships, shipbuilding and docks, as well as lions' heads in the upper lights (see Plate 58). At Hexham, the North British Arms (now Rockin' Horse), Station Road has a pair of windows embossed with the now irrelevant arms of the North British Railway, as well as a single window with a floral design.

The Crown Posada (previously the Crown) in Newcastle's Side boasts the best stained glass windows in the area; the pub itself was rebuilt in 1880 for local brewer John Sanderson, but the glass, showing almost Pre-Raphaelite figures, was a later addition. Sunderland's Mountain Daisy has good stained glass windows in the rear buffet showing scenes of eating and drinking, and the same subject is portrayed in the top lights of the Cleveland Arms, on the corner of York Street and Cleveland Street, Albert Hill, Darlington. This slightly art nouveau work includes some painted glass (see Col. Plate 15). Donneky's, Ryhope Street, Ryhope has an elegant

58. *Ship in the Hole*

Newcastle, is now on display in the Museum of Science and Engineering, Blandford Square, Newcastle. The pub has been demolished but the glass is in fine condition, the painting being the centre of a bright stained glass window.

The most unusual window in the north east billows out from the front of the Brewers Arms, Marygate, Berwick-upon-Tweed (see Plate 60). As the mosaic in the doorway informs the customer, the pub once sold the beer of Thomas and James Bernard Ltd. of Edinburgh, and since mosaic, facade and window seem contemporaneous, it is likely that this curving glass extravaganza is the work of their unknown designer; it probably dates from the early twentieth century, and served to entice the drinker into the long, narrow interior.

59. *Stanley Arms*

top light of leaded glass showing a blue bell, doubtless a clue as to the pub's original name.

The effectiveness of the combination of painted and stained glass is shown by the fanlight of the Stanley Arms, Stanley Street, North Shields, an original remnant in an otherwise completely modernised pub. The central painted glass panel is an excellent depiction of a paddle steamer, this rectangle being surrounded by a loose art nouveau cartouche of leaded glass panels (see Plate 59). The painted glass picture of blast furnaces, which used to decorate the Blast Furnace Inn, Scotswood Road,

60. Brewers Arms

12. Black Swan

THE INTERIOR

Once drawn through the inner porch doors and into the pub, the drinker would be confronted by the bar counter, the functional basis of the pub. Although sometimes divided into separate sections by wood and glass screens, the massive counter dominated the bar, aided by the back fitting which rose in tiers of shelves and columns to a pediment. The typical north eastern bar counter had an S-shaped profile towards the drinking area, the polished mahogany top resting on the flat of the S with the counter bulging out beneath it and then curving back nearer ground level. The counter would be ornamented with carving, often decorated pilasters. Less lavishly fitted-out bars had a mahogany counter top resting

13. Black Swan

on a planked support with a solid wooden base. In the north east the back fitting, necessary for storing and displaying bottles and glasses, is normally of the shelves and pediment variety rather than the overmantel style popular in London in the 1890s. These were based on the Victorian fireplace surround, and offered space for showing off artistic objects as well as the usual bottles.

There are few interiors which have survived intact from the nineteenth or early twentieth century, the most frequent casualties having been the wood and glass screens which divided up the long bars, and the snob screens which stood on the counter partially separating publican and customer. The screens which demarcated parts of the bar area were sometimes replaced by continuous wood panelling to give small cubicles (rather like family pews in a Georgian church) instead of roughly delimited spaces for public bars or snugs. The effect was of a series of shoulder height wooden boxes arranged around the bar counter. This compartmentalised arrangement was fashionable in London around 1890, but although bar space in urban north eastern pubs was frequently divided into a number of smaller areas in the early 1890s, this trend does not seem to have either followed from an earlier use of cubicles or led to their introduction. One great and wonderfully preserved exception to this rule is the Free Trade Inn, Castlegate, Berwick-upon-Tweed, which has a far finer array of boxes than any of the few extant London examples. Cubicles were certainly found in many Scottish pubs in the late nineteenth century, before the licensing authorities caused their removal to allow increased supervision of drinkers, and the Free Trade Inn follows this Scottish pattern rather than the more open Northumbrian style.

By the turn of the century the general arrangement of bar space in north eastern pubs resembled that of the Scottish pubs, then minus their cubicles, rather than the lay-out of southern English pubs. The typical Newcastle pub would by then have had a single large bar partially subdivided by two or three screens, with a sitting room to the rear. In London, there were more and smaller bars within each pub, and the divisions between bars were more rigid; in contrast, the newly opened up Scottish pubs had just a few dividing screens.

One of the best preserved interiors in Northumbria is that of the Victoria in Hallgarth Street, Durham, an Oswald pub designed for local innkeepers J. A. Lumsden & Co. in 1898. Its outstanding feature is a complete screened family department at the rear of the corner public bar, which also has the upper part of its back fitting, an unusual partially enclosed shelf with a miniature balustrade. The Oswald practice estimated the cost of the pub at £1240, which included a Cuba mahogany counter top and the carved stone cartouche on the front elevation, showing the building date (1899) and the head of a youthful Queen Victoria.

Small pubs have often retained more of their original fittings than the large city centre houses, although some of the exceptions such as Sunderland's Dun Cow and its superb back fitting have already been mentioned. Another excellent small scale interior is that of the Globe, Battle Hill, Hexham, with its restrained, semi-kidney-shaped bar counter. Its back fitting curves out from the wall and is supported by a central scrolled bracket, and there is also a bar screen and some good glasswork. The Colpitts Hotel, Hawthorn Terrace, Durham has a fine panelled and pilastered bar counter dating from the 1890s as well as a tall back bar fitting with narrow shelves, designed to fit the tiny serving area. Darlington's Cleveland Arms has a hefty panelled bar counter but the back fitting is a delicate miniature with mirrors reflecting the stained glass of the window, its shelves topped with a plump ball finial. Newcastle's Big Lamp brewery, responsible for the botched 'improvement' of the Wheatsheaf in

Felling, modernised the Cleveland Arms in summer 1988, only to sell it a few months later.

In Newcastle, the Newcastle Arms, Darn Crook retains its original counter, back fitting, some embossed glass and, best of all, a screen complete with glass which effectively turns the bay window area of the bar into a separate room. This is an Oswald pub, designed in 1902 for wine and spirit merchants Richard Charlton Ltd. The most evocative interior in Newcastle is probably that of the Hydraulic Crane on the Scotswood Road, designed in 1900 for Arrols by B. F. Simpson. The pub went through rebuilding and a series of alterations before 1900, but its present state gives a good impression of the manner in which areas of a large bar could be screened off to provide snug drinking niches. The counter, back fitting, fire surrounds and some glasswork are original, the (later) glass in the Scotswood Road doors being particularly good. Also in Newcastle the Cackett and Burns Dick designed Bridge Hotel has a fine interior, vandalised in 1988 when the snob screens were removed. Finally the Villa Victoria on Westmorland Road still has most of its original counter, some painted glass and relief wallpaper; the pub, then the Victoria Cottage, was rebuilt in 1893 by B. F. Simpson, although parts of the interior date from the 1931 alterations carried out for Duncan & Daglish.

Although most pub interiors were decorated by local craftsmen using a combination of carved wood, embossed and brilliant cut glass, mirrors and relief wallpaper, occasionally and dramatically ceramic tiles took the place of wood and wallpaper on counter and walls. The 1880s and 1890s saw a great increase in demand for easily cleaned, hard wearing ceramic tiles, which were used in both housing and public buildings. Many new firms began to mass produce tiles in the 1870s-1890s, and builders and architects selected designs from the range of stock shown in their catalogues. Tile panels could also be hand painted, and the back bar of the Mountain Daisy, Hylton Road, Sunderland has a wonderful array of painted panels, mass produced tiles and faience, the ceramics completely covering both counter and walls (see Plate 61). The panels, measuring 3ft. by 4ft. 6ins., show local scenes including Cragside, Bamburgh Castle, Marsden Rock, Durham Cathedral and the bridges of Newcastle and Sunderland. The counter, a quarter circle, is faced with yellow and green faience slabs in a pattern of animal heads and swags. The overall effect of the colourful panels and shining faience is striking, and all the work is still in excellent condition. It was carried out by the firm of Craven Dunnill & Co. of Jackfield in the Ironbridge Gorge, Shropshire (who also produced the tile panel of the North Eastern Railway network which can be seen on Tynemouth Station). The company was established in 1871 and quickly became a rival to Maw & Co., then the leading tile manufacturers; by the turn of the century Craven Dunnill tiles were being used in all parts of Britain and the Empire. Their more important works, listed in their catalogues, included Manchester Town Hall, Chester Cathedral and the refreshment room at Snow Hill Station, Birmingham. The illustration of the Mountain Daisy appeared in their own album of record photographs, which featured another 14 pubs and hotels, as well as Charlton's Restaurant in Newcastle.

The only comparable work in the north east is

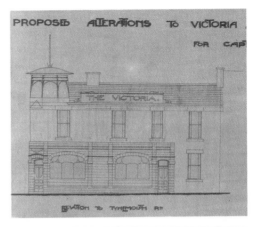

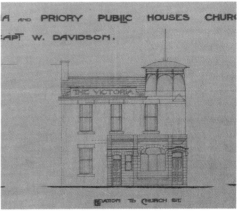

14. *Far left, top: Railway Hotel*
15. *Far left, below: Cleveland Arms*
16. *Left. Detail of refreshment room faience work,*
Newcastle Central Station
17. *Above: Victoria/Tap and Spile, Tynemouth Road,*
North Shields,
August 1900 plans and elevation by
J. W. Wardle, not built (NTPD)

the refreshment room of Newcastle Central Station, which recently served as a buffet and bar (with consequent alterations) but is currently awaiting a new use. It is decorated from floor to ceiling with Burmantofts faience in Baroque style, including high relief animal heads and flowers. The columns are particularly impressive even though some of the faience has been overpainted (see Col. Plate 16). It is to be hoped that this glorious piece of work can be restored to its former splendour when the room is eventually brought back into use.

With faience facades and painted tile panels, towering gables and convoluted back fittings, the Victorian and Edwardian pubs of the north east were as richly decorated as those of the more publicised London area, if not as large or as great in number. The idiosyncrasies of design which typify the pubs of each town and city make the Northumbrian pub at the turn of the century a particularly interesting building form. The post-First World War pubs, the reformed pubs devised by brewers and architects to placate the licensing justices and attract the family into garden and dining room, were less diverse. However, even the inter-war climate of hostility towards drinking in Victorian luxury and comfort did not prevent a few Northumbrian architects producing interesting and unusual pubs.

THE REFORMED PUB

The inter-war pub came in two basic styles, neo-Tudor and neo-Georgian. Neo-Georgian was popular on the growing 1930s housing estates of Newcastle

61. Left: Back bar of the Mountain Daisy,
Hylton Road, Sunderland
(Ironbridge Gorge Museum Trust)

and its coastal fringe from Monkseaton to North Shields, the typical design being a two storey stuccoed brick box with imitation quoins, with or without a portico. The Foxhunters, Rake Lane, Preston and the Collingwood Arms, Front Street, Chirton are both on this pattern, which was an attempt to introduce ideas of respectability and openness into the public house by means of an architectural interpretation of classical Georgian virtues. These pubs were large, and often sited on main roads to attract the increasing amount of private car trade; the Three Mile Inn (1936), Great North Road, Gosforth and the Waggon Team (1938), Lobley Hill Road, Lobley Hill with its tetrastyle portico are good examples of this roadhouse style.

Neo-Tudor or brewers' Tudor was used for the new estate pubs of the 1930s but was also capable of expansion for even larger sites such as that of the butterfly plan Marsden Inn (1938), Prince Edward Road, Marsden, South Shields. The butterfly plan, designed to make the best use of the sun, had first been used for Edwardian country houses and became fashionable again in the 1930s when sunshine and the open air were in vogue. The juxtaposition of the contemporary butterfly plan with a neo-Tudor elevation, designed to recall Olde England, coaching inns and roaring fires was incongruous but a pragmatic success. The Banks o' the Tyne (1921), Wagonway Road, Hebburn is an early example of neo-Tudor, small in comparison with the Northumbria in Prudhoe, the red brick Albion on The Village, Ryhope, or the White Horse, Harrowgate Hill, Darlington. The White Horse is a much less convincing version of the genre dating from 1951, by which time the brewers had generally

62. New Tyne Iron

given up on Tudor as a symbol of clean living and resorted to a smaller modern brick vernacular. An interesting estate pub in neo-Tudor is the Newton Park Hotel, Benton Road, Newcastle, which retains two original doorcases and a chimney-stack with brick tumbling (bricks laid diagonally as an ornamental device). Its interior has magnificent relief floral patterned ceiling papers in both the main bar and the billiard room.

The inter-war years were not completely dominated by the brewers' stylistic conservatism. The Milburns' Seaburn Hotel (1937), Queens Parade, Whitburn is a modern movement essay with classical motifs, while the Lambton Worm, North Road, Chester-le-street, is an almost perfect white modernist pub complete with curving suntrap windows and original glazing bars. The effect is

spoiled only by a pitched roof; modern movement theory demanded a flat roof for sun worship. Seaside hotels were more likely candidates for modern movement treatment than inland pubs, as the new style became associated with fresh air, sun, travel and speed; the white, flat roofed hotel might have been out of place in the city but could be attractive at the seaside. The Lambton Worm is a real oddity in this respect, masquerading as a traditional design with a pitched roof.

Most interesting of all the reformed pubs is the New Tyne Iron, situated at the western end of the Scotswood Road, Lemington (see Plate 62). It was designed in 1936 by South Shields architect Howard Hill for Bernards of Edinburgh, already noted for their Brewers Arms in Berwick with its unusual glazing. It can best be described as a Moderne pub, a watered down version of Art Deco which took on some of its 'jazz' decorative characteristics but did not use every element in the building to achieve an Art Deco effect. The pediments on the doorcases of both side wings are typical of the Art Deco style, and the corner glazing in the upper storey is also indicative of the building date (1937), but there is now nothing left of the original interior which had a severely functional arrangement of central service area surrounded by bar, sitting room, dining room and kitchen.

A matt faience (Marmo or a similar brand name) was sometimes used for refacing pubs between the wars. At the Fighting Cocks in Crossgate, Durham the ground floor and part of the first floor have been refaced in a cream unglazed faience, complete with a pair of moulded fighting cocks. The building's timber frame construction is visible in its west gable end, but sits rather oddly with the 1920s/30s refacing in neo-Georgian style; a potted history of architecture in a single pub. The interior of the outwardly slightly modernist Scrogg, Scrogg Road, Walker provides a glorious Art Deco finale to the 1940s, coming before the hectic stylistic changes of post-Second World War theme pub interiors. In the lounge bar, a central column weirdly disguised as a palm tree supports a horizontal circular top light about 20ft. in diameter, glazed with mainly yellow stained glass.

After the extremes of Art Deco and the gigantism of neo-Georgian and neo-Tudor, post-Second World War pubs initially lacked decorative direction. Brewery mergers from the mid-1950s onwards produced a highly competitive industry in which individuality was less favoured than a consistent national image as a means of attracting customers. House architects and house style took over from local idiosyncrasy, and pubs were refurbished and given themes rather than simply being decorated. The materials in use reflected the lack of craft skills available, and the pub itself became a mass produced object. Theme pubs were devised for younger customers, now consumers, and the national brewery companies pressed ahead with improvements which certainly made pubs more comfortable, warmer and safer places, but also disposed of all reminders of the Victorian heyday of the pub. Currently, new pub design is low profile vernacular, typified by the red brick Shieling on the Beaumont Park estate in Monkseaton, or refurbished Victorian using architectural salvage to provide extra genuine artefacts. Perhaps the resurgence of small breweries and craft skills (and growing signs of architectural revolution) will combine to produce a 1990s decorative pub boom, with pubs as showpieces of arts and crafts; economics, as ever, will be the deciding factor.

CHAPTER ELEVEN

The Northumbrian Pub

IS there any such thing as a typical Northumbrian pub? If the pub simply reflects the local townscape or landscape then perhaps not, as the counties of Northumbria are immensely varied, including everything from bleak uninhabited moors to highly populated urban areas, from seaside resorts to model villages. But the pub is more than just a building in a landscape; it is the sum of social, economic and artistic forces working on brewers, architects and builders. These forces may be national (architectural trends) or local (availability of skilled craftsmen), but their combination results in buildings which bear the marks of their place of origin as well as having a recognisable national identity as public houses. Only where long term influences on the building form are overriding, as in the countryside where building materials are restricted to those locally available, is the pub just another building; in the urban north east the pub is special.

The Northumbrian country pub certainly has a specific building form, but apart from the details of the building materials, it is not unlike the country pub in any other part of England. It is a vernacular building, constructed of local stone (probably sandstone), a two or three storey Georgian house now bearing the marks of nearly two centuries of accretion and alteration. Its ground floor has been opened out to accommodate the necessary bars and modern seating arrangements, but it is still recognisably a building in keeping with the slowly changing townscape. There is no strong statement of identity, the pub is simply an inconspicuous part of the town or village it serves. It would be wrong to select one pub as being the epitome of the Northumbrian country pub, but the Black Bull at Etal is as typical in its building form and atypical in its building material (a thatched roof) as any in Northumbria; it is completely of the region, but could be from the deep south of England.

In the large town or city the appearance of the pub began to matter to brewer, to landlord and to customer, around the end of the nineteenth century. What could the publican provide for the potential customer which would be dramatically different from the wares on offer at any other pub? Very little but atmosphere. Architects and builders were employed to produce magical, theatrical buildings to seduce the customer, towering four and five storey monsters for the city centres but more often bright and colourful corner pubs for the thriving industrial towns. It is the small but highly decorative pub which is typical of the north east, with a Baroque faience exterior and an interior displaying intricate joinery produced by local craftsmen. These pubs are ordinary but distinctive, high quality buildings which could not be mistaken for any other building type. The County in Walker, the Duke of Wellington in Howdon and, best of all, the Wheatsheaf in Felling are prime examples of north eastern small pub architecture, functioning today much as they did when originally built. Also a working pub, but rebuilt at the North of England Open Air Museum in Beamish, Co. Durham, after being removed from its previous site in Bishop Auckland is the Sun Inn, with a fine Victorian interior.

The pub architects of the late Victorian and Edwardian period were men who had wide general practices but specialised in pubs as a result of initial contacts with brewers or wine and spirit merchants on small jobs; as the brewing industry expanded around the turn of the century, so did the scale of their pub work. Stylistically, most pub architects adopted a similar approach during the pub building boom: for city pubs, a bubbling Baroque which included all manner of towers, domes, drums, oriels and bay windows, succeeded by elegant Art Nouveau forms and later a touch of neo-Georgian. Smaller pubs were dominated more by materials than design elements, as with the use of faience facades. Simpson and the Milburns were more outrageous designers than the Oswalds, although the interiors produced by the Oswald practice (detailed drawings still exist) are superlative; it is difficult to say how much other pub interior work was produced by architects rather than craftsmen, as there are few records.

Most turn of the century architects would have been capable of turning out a pub, probably in any style desired by the client, and it is the occasional pub architects who have given us some of the most unusual pubs. John Spencer's Wolsington House in North Shields and Henry Grieves' Scotia in South Shields are but two examples, followed in the thirties by Howard Hill's New Tyne Iron on the Scotswood Road. Sadly, the strangest pub in north east England was never built; it was a design for the rebuilding of the Victoria and Priory public houses, situated side by side on the Tynemouth Road in North Shields. The architect was Joseph W. Wardle of South Shields, who later produced the fantastic faience facade for the Albert in Hebburn. For the new Victoria, in August 1900 he proposed a startling blue and yellow Art Nouveau elevation (see Col. Plate 17). The ground floor would probably have been faced with faience, as well as part of the corner tower with its elegantly curved glazing bars. The owner, one Captain Davidson, perhaps could not afford the expense of such a design, as it was never built despite receiving approval from the Sanitary Authority. The pubs remained as they were, the end houses of a terrace, until enlargement by Camerons in 1934. Ironically the Victoria is now one of the Tap and Spile chain of Camerons pubs, but in their attempt to recreate a cosy drinking environment they have produced only a neutral though comfortable interior, with the exterior unchanged; Wardle's design would have been far more exciting!

The surviving urban pubs of Northumbria are a tribute to the skills of nineteenth and early twentieth century architects and craftsmen. Enough original interiors remain to demonstrate their luxurious quality, and the exteriors, even of small pubs, are colourful and architecturally delightful elements of the townscape. Of course, many pubs built in the boom years have been demolished, and even more interiors have been replaced as fashions swung away from heavy Victorian through thirties streamlining and the modernist fifties to the functionalism of the sixties. Neo-Victorian is the current vogue for pub interiors, using original materials where possible (redundant churches are a fruitful source), even including the architect's plans. The newly refurbished Adelphi in Shakespeare Street, Newcastle has a copy of its original plan decorating the interior, while outside a line of giant lamps illuminates the ground floor facade.

Pub design and decoration will never again reach the heights of the Edwardian years because the cost would be forbidding, even if the skills and materials were still available. Competition in the brewing industry, one of the factors behind the building boom of the 1890s and 1900s, is as intense in the 1980s with chains of pubs being sold and resold between multinational companies whose main interests are no longer solely within the drink trade. Ownership of public houses is still equated with profitability, but it is unlikely that the takeover activity will lead to many more pubs being built, as refurbishing is a cheaper alternative (although energy costs often increase as a result). While Victoriana is fashionable, the Northumbrian pub heritage is probably safe, although prone to accidental destruction through piecemeal 'improvements', but when the opulence of the Victorian or Edwardian drinking house becomes less chic, and thus less lucrative, then some fine locals may be in danger.

Brewers have yet to realise that history can be extremely profitable, and that they own buildings capable of showing off the very best of the architectural and craft skills of nearly a century ago; for once, the restoration of good buildings and the search for profit could be complementary. The 1988 relaxation of the licensing laws may encourage both large brewing conglomerates and the rapidly increasing number of small independent brewers to rethink traditional methods of selling beer, to occasionally abandon bland refurbishment and instead to encourage a celebration of local life and craft skills through their buildings. Doubtless many pubs will always be anonymous places to drink, but the interests of brewer and customer alike demand that this is not the case everywhere. The Victorian pub was glamorous, colourful, sparkling and different from other buildings. Fortunately the Northumbrian pub is still different and still functioning; no need for museums when buildings are used, useful and enjoyed.

BIBLIOGRAPHY

The main sources of information for this book were the pubs themselves and the related archival material which is held by the various record offices. The architectural history of the public house has now become a relatively popular topic, but most previous work on north eastern pubs has been largely anecdotal. In contrast, the brewing industry has been studied in depth, and I have relied greatly on Donnachie's 'A history of the brewing industry in Scotland', and 'The brewing industry' by Hawkins and Pass for background data. Barber's 'Where have all the breweries gone?' is an excellent source for brewery history, and the Journal of the Brewery History Society is also useful, though tending to concentrate on southern breweries. For information on north eastern brewers, Chilton and Poppleston's paper (obtainable in Local Studies, Newcastle upon Tyne City Library) is the best available work.

ARCHITECTS

1. CORFE, TOM (ed.), 1983, The buildings of Sunderland 1814- 1914, Tyne and Wear County Council Museums.
2. DENDY, F. W., 1930, A memoir of the late Joseph Oswald, Archaeologia Aeliana, vol 7, 4th series, pp 179- 183.
3. GETTINGS, LEONARD, 1976, Benjamin Ferdinand Simpson 1890- 1910, unpub. BA thesis, Jan, Univ. of Newcastle upon Tyne School of Architecture.
4. THOMPSON, G. C. W., 1977, SEPTIMUS OSWALD 1823- 1894, unpub. BA dissertation, Jan, Univ. of Newcastle upon Tyne School of Architecture.
5. OBIT: JAMES T. CACKETT, RIBA Journal, 14 April 1928, 3rd series, vol 35, no 11, p 375.
6. OBIT: JOSEPH OSWALD, Newcastle Daily Journal, 15 January 1930, p 11.

ARCHITECTURAL CERAMICS

1. HERBERT, A. T., 1979, Jackfield decorative tiles in use, Industrial Archaeology Review, vol 3, no 2, Spring, pp 146- 152.
2. IRVINE, LOUISE, 1981, The decorative spirit, The Conoisseur, Dec, vol 208, no 838, pp 272-5.
3. VAN LEMMEN, HANS, 1983, Burmantoft's Marmo, Glazed Expressions, Summer, pp 1-2.
4. VAN LEMMEN, HANS, 1981, Victorian tiles, Shire Publications, Princes Risborough.
5. STEWART, G. T., 1973, Victorian faience, unpub. ms., North Shields.
6. STRATTON, MICHAEL, 1986, The terracotta industry, Industrial Archaeology Review, Spring, vol 8, no 2, pp 194- 214.

ARCHITECTURAL HISTORY - PUBLIC HOUSES

1. BINNEY, MARCUS and MILNE, EMMA (eds), 1983, Time gentlemen please!, SAVE/CAMRA, SAVE, London.
2. BRABBS, DERRY, 1986, English country pubs, Weidenfeld and Nicolson, London.
3. COOPER, ANDREW, HAMMOND, CHRIS and HOWARD, JON, 1985, Survey of Leeds public houses, Victorian Society, West Yorkshire Group, Journal, pp 5-26.
4. CRAWFORD, ALAN, DUNN, MICHAEL and THORNE, ROBERT, 1986, Birmingham pubs 1880-1939, Alan Sutton Publishing, Gloucester. (Also previous ed., Birmingham, 1975.)
5. CURL, JAMES STEVENS, 1972, The vanished gin palaces, Country Life, 22 June, vol 151, no 3914, pp 1598-1600.
6. ELWALL, ROBERT, 1983, Bricks and beer, English pub architecture 1830-1939, British Architectural Library, London.

7. GIROUARD, MARK, 1984, Victorian pubs, Yale University Press, London (first pub. 1975).
8. GIROUARD, MARK, 1977, Sweetness and light, OUP, Oxford.
9. HARRISON, BRIAN, 1973, Pubs, pp 161-190 in H. J. Dyos and Michael Wolff (eds), The Victorian city, vol 1, RKP, London.
10. RICHARDSON, A. E., 1934, The old inns of England, Batsford, London.
11. English inns, 1951, Odhams Press, London.

BREWING INDUSTRY

1. BARBER, NORMAN, c1982, Where have all the breweries gone?, Neil Richardson/CAMRA, Swinton.
2. DONNACHIE, IAN, 1979, A history of the brewing industry in Scotland, John Donald, Edinburgh.
3. GOURVISH, T. R. and WILSON, R. G., 1985, Profitability in the brewing industry, 1885-1914, Business History, July, vol 27, no 2, pp 146-165.
4. HAWKINS, K. H. and PASS, C. L., 1979, The brewing industry, Heinemann, London.
5. KNOX, D. M., 1958, The development of the tied house system in London, Oxford Economic Papers, Feb, NS vol 10, no 1, pp 66-83.
6. MARK, JOHN, 1985, Changes in the British brewing industry in the twentieth century, pp 81-101 in Derek J. Oddy and Derek S. Miller (eds), Diet and health in modern Britain, Croom Helm, London.

GOVERNMENT PUBLICATIONS

BPP = British Parliamentary Papers
1. BPP 1852-53, XXXVII.1, Select Committee on public houses and places of entertainment.
2. BPP 1852-53, LXXXI.295, Drunkenness etc.
3. BPP 1877, LXIX.291, Drunkenness etc.
4. BPP 1890, LXIII.65, Returns of licences.
5. BPP 1890-1, LXVIII.123, On-licences return.
6. BPP 1890-1, LXXVII.61, Return relating to brewers' licences.
7. BPP 1892, LXVIII.147, On-licence returns.
8. BPP 1897, XXXIV.253, Royal Commission on the liquor licensing laws, Evidence, vol 1.
9. BPP 1898, XXXVI.9, Royal Commission on the liquor licensing laws, Evidence, vol 3.

NORTH EASTERN BREWING INDUSTRY

1. BENNISON, BRIAN, 1985, The socio-economic factors underlying the emergence of early twentieth century cooperative brewing: with particular reference to the north east of England, Paper presented at Annual Conference of the Association of Polytechnic Teachers of Economics, 1-4 April.
2. CHILTON, PETER and POPPLESTON, MICHAEL, c1978, History of brewers in north east England, typescript.
3. MERRINGTON, JIM and BROWN, ANDREW, Two hundred years of Newcastle ales, Part 1, Autumn 1970, The Essandenn, no 22, pp 4-8, Part 2, Winter 1970-71, The Essandenn, no 23, pp 8- 12.
4. WEBB, J. M., 1975, Vaux Breweries - 100 years at Castle Street, Things that affect us (Vaux house journal), Spring, no 90, pp 6-12.

NORTH EASTERN HISTORY

1. CORFE, TOM, 1973, Sunderland, A short history, Frank Graham, Newcastle.
2. HAYWOOD, PETER, 1984, Around Felling High Street, Gateshead MBC.
3. HOOLE, K., 1974, A regional history of the railways of Great Britain, vol IV, The north east, David & Charles, Newton Abbot.
4. McCORD, NORMAN, 1979, North east England, Batsford, London.
5. MACKENZIE, E., 1827, A descriptive and historical account of the town and county of Newcastle upon Tyne, Mackenzie and Dent, Newcastle.
6. Northumberland Record Office, 1969, Northumberland railways from 1700, NRO, Newcastle.

7. TURNBULL, LES, 1987, The history of lead mining in the north east of England, Sandhill Press, Alnwick.
8. Tyne and Wear County Council Museums, 1979, Glassmaking on Wearside.

NORTH EASTERN PUBS

1. ALDERSON, I. S., 1975, The public houses, Things that affect us (Vaux house journal), Spring, no 90, pp 23-31.
2. BEAN, DAVID, 1971, Tyneside, A biography, Macmillan, London.
3. BOWER, M. E., 1978, The evolution of the public house, unpub. BA dissertation, Jan, Univ. of Newcastle upon Tyne School of Architecture.
4. BUCKLEY, CHERYL and WALKER, LYNNE, 1982, Between the wars, Architecture and design on Tyneside 1919-1939, Newcastle upon Tyne Polytechnic.
5. GIBSON, PETER, 1985, Southwick-on-Wear, Southwick Publications, Sunderland.
6. GRAHAM, FRANK, 1977, The old halls, houses and inns of Northumberland, Frank Graham, Newcastle.
7. HANSON, NEIL (ed), 1987, Good beer guide 1988, CAMRA, St Albans.
8. MILBURN, T. A., 1987, Life and times in Weardale 1840-1910, Weardale Museum, Ireshopeburn.
9. Newcastle City Libraries, 1988, Scotswood Road Pubs, Newcastle.
10. Newcastle Daily Journal, 1902, Earl Grey's Trust Scheme, 28 Jan, p 5.
11. Northumbria Tourist Board, 1970?, Some interesting inns and taverns, NTB, Newcastle.
12. Weardale Press, 1968, Historic and new inns of interest, Weardale Press, Halifax.
13. -----, c1966, The Marine Grotto, Marsden, Vaux Breweries, Sunderland.

PUB DESIGN

1. JOHNSON, W. Branch, 1955, The inn as a community centre, The Amateur Historian, Apr/May, vol 2, no 5, pp 134-7.
2. NAIRN, IAN and BROWNE, KENNETH, 1962, Pub in focus, Architectural Review (AR), Dec, vol 132, no 790, pp 401-4.
3. OLIVER, BASIL, 1947, The renaissance of the English public house, Faber, London.
4. PIPER, JOHN, 1940, Fully licensed, AR, Mar, vol 87, pp 87-100.
5. SPILLER, BRIAN, 1955, Brewers' house styles, AR, Dec, vol 118, no 708, pp 372-381.
6. WYKEHAM, HUGH, 1958, The face of the pub, AR, Dec, vol 124, no 743, pp 366-373.
7. -----, 1988, High energy pubs: the bitter truth, Architects' Journal, 7 Sept, vol 187, no 36, p 12.

SOURCES

1. FAULKNER, N. O., 1988, Allied Breweries, A long life, Allied Breweries Ltd, History Project, London.
2. ROWE, D. J. (ed), 1979, Northern Business Histories, A bibliography, Library Association, London.

TEMPERANCE AND LICENSING

1. ASKWITH, LORD, 1928, British taverns, Routledge, London.
2. BAILEY, PETER, 1987, Leisure and class in Victorian England, Methuen, London, (first pub. 1978).
3. CUNNINGHAM, HUGH, 1980, Leisure in the industrial revolution, St Martin's Press, New York.
4. HARRISON, BRIAN, 1971, Drink and the Victorians, Faber, London.
5. THORNE, ROBERT, 1985, The movement for public house reform 1892-1914, pp 231-254 in Derek J. Oddy and Derek S. Miller (eds), Diet and health in modern Britain, Croom Helm, London.
6. WEIR, R. B., 1984, Obsessed with moderation, British Journal of Addiction, vol 79, pp 93-107.
7. WILSON, GEORGE B., 1940, Alcohol and the nation, Nicholson and Watson, London.

Architects known to have built, rebuilt or altered a pub mentioned in the text are listed below, together with the date of the relevant design.

JAMES T. CACKETT (and R. BURNS DICK)
    1898 Cumberland Arms, Byker
    1898 Millstone, South Gosforth
    1900 White Hart, Newcastle upon Tyne
    1901 Bridge Hotel, Newcastle upon Tyne
GEORGE COOPER
    1903 Hole in the Wall, Darlington
DIXON & SONS
    1947 Rose and Crown, Bellingham
JOHN DOBSON
    1830 Mitre, Benwell
J. WARDLE DONALD
    1896 Britannia, South Shields
    1900 Duke of Cumberland, Newcastle upon Tyne
ARTHUR GIBSON
    1885 Vine, Newcastle upon Tyne
JOHN GIBSON
    1878 Punch Bowl, Jesmond
HENRY GRIEVES
    1903 Scotia, South Shields
F. R. N. HASWELL
    1898, 1934 Cumberland Arms, Tynemouth
    1898 Garricks Head, North Shields
    1905, 1930 Turks Head, Tynemouth
    1913 Borough Arms, North Shields
HUGH HEDLEY
    1901 Londonderry, Sunderland
    1906 Tram Car, Southwick, Sunderland
HOWARD HILL
    1936 New Tyne Iron, Newcastle upon Tyne
WILLIAM HOPE & J. C. MAXWELL
    1901 Bath Hotel, Tynemouth
W. & T. R. MILBURN
    1897 Porthole, North Shields
    1901 Mountain Daisy, Sunderland
    1902 Bells, Sunderland

    1903 Hat and Feather, Sunderland
    1937 Seaburn Hotel, Whitburn
T. H. MURRAY
    1904 Kings Head, Wolsingham
OSWALD PRACTICE
    1890, 1896 Addison, Heaton
    1891, 1900 Berwick Arms, North Shields
    1891 Duke of Argyle, Newcastle upon Tyne
    1892 Albion, North Shields
    1893 Cumberland Grill, South Shields
    1894 Grey Bull, Morpeth
    1894, 1908 Half Moon, Durham
    1894, 1897,1910 Railway, North Shields
    1895 Free Trade, Byker
    1897 Blyth and Tyne, North Shields
    1897-8 Wheat Sheaf, Roker, Sunderland
    1898 Victoria, Durham
    1900-1 Blue Bell, Roker, Sunderland
    1901, 1908 Vine, Newcastle upon Tyne
    1902 Bee Hive, Newcastle upon Tyne
    1902 Newcastle Arms, Newcastle upon Tyne
    1902 Phoenix, North Shields
    1904 Chain Locker, North Shields
    1905 Old Hawk, Byker
    1930 Percy Arms, Tynemouth
    1934 Duke of Wellington, Kenton
    1939 Green Tree, Benwell
    1930s Foxhunters, Preston, North Shields
    1930s Railway, Walker
    1930s Ship, Whitley Bay
JAMES PAINE
    1755-64 Border Minstrel, High Gosforth Park
BENJAMIN F. SIMPSON (and SIDNEY H. LAWSON)
    1891 Golden Lion, Byker
    1892 Lord Chancellor, Newcastle upon Tyne
    1893 Villa Victoria, Newcastle upon Tyne
    1896 Lord Clyde, Byker
    1898 Cumberland Arms, Byker
    1899 Beeswing, Felling
    1899 Lambs Arms, West Ryton

1899 Royal Turf, Felling
1900 Hydraulic Crane, Newcastle upon Tyne
1901 Bay Horse, Felling
1901 Dun Cow, Sunderland
1903 Grey Horse, Sunderland
1903 Half Moon, Newcastle upon Tyne
1903 Half Moon, Sunderland
1913 Gosforth Hotel, Gosforth
1914 Rose and Crown, Newcastle upon Tyne
1928 Old George, Newcastle upon Tyne
1938 Black Bull, Bellingham
JOHN SPENCER
    1900-1 Wolsington House, North Shields

DAVID STEPHENSON
    1806-17 Northumberland Arms, North Shields
ARTHUR STOCKWELL
    1897 Fighting Cocks, Byker
    1900 Brandling Villa, South Gosforth
JOSEPH W. WARDLE
    1900 Victoria, North Shields
    1908 Albert, Hebburn
WATSON
    1902 Coach and Horses, Wallsend
T. K. WHITE and S. J. STEPHENSON
    1906 County Hotel, Walker

ARCHITECTURAL TERMS

1. Rusticated Quoins
2. Quoins
3. Deep Semi Circular Window
4. Cornice
5. Dentil
6. Egg and Dart
7. Cupola
8. Fleche
9. Ogee Dome
10. Open Drum
11. Ball Finial
12. Pediment
13. Dutch Gable
14. Shaped Gable
15. Dormer Window
16. Oriel Window
17. Chamfered Corner
18. Swag
19. Canopy
20. Fluted Corinthian Column
21. Fanlight
22. Cartouche
23. Giant Ionic Pilaster
24. Architrave
25. Venetian Window
26. Frieze
27. Fret Pattern
28. Spandrel
29. Plinth
30. Shop Front Style
31. Top Lights.

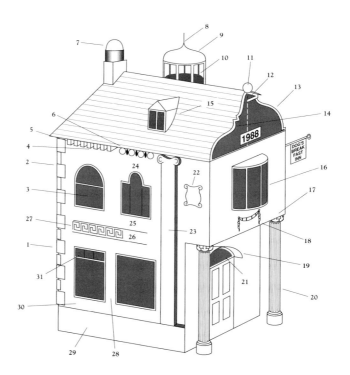